The Chickenfried Café

A Novel

By John Purner

ISBN-13: 978-0692337974
ISBN-10: 0692337970

For quantity discounts on volume orders please contact

$100 Hamburger Publishing
PO Box 915441
Longwood, FL 32791-5441

Internet: www.100dollarhamburger.com
Email: pirep@100dollarhamburger.com

First Printing: November 2014

Cover photo credit: Renee Purner/www.photos-by-renee.com

Table of Contents

Departure

"It takes equal measures of science and art to turn a piece of beef better suited for shoe leather into **chickenfried steak**. Creating a successful restaurant at a country airport and serving nothing but that savory morsel requires a sorcerer's book of spells and a magic wand. You, Milton Muzny (*Mooooz knee*) have accomplished this feat twenty seven times in just three years. I'm eager to learn how you did it?

Let's begin with the not so obvious '*where*' question. La Grange, Texas seems an odd pick for location number one?"

"Placing the flagship here wasn't an act of choice, Ms. Muckelroy. The decision sprang from unbridled faith, fashioned by an appetite favoring airplanes, chickenfried steak and golf, laced with a dash of '*nowhere else to go*'.

If it suits you, ma'am, I'll tell the tale from the middle as the beginning happened far too long ago to be remembered and the end is closer than I care to contemplate."

"Start where you like, Mr. Muzny, and take as long as necessary. I'll just turn on my recorder. It makes my work easier, assures accuracy and allows me to focus on your every word."

"I'll start mine as well, just in case." *(A lifelong paranoid, Milton, didn't trust most people, particularly those with 'reporter' stamped on their business card.)*

So tell me, Angela Muckelroy, why has **Sports Illustrated** sent such a distinguished reporter as you to interview me? I thought you'd be better suited for doing a story for the swimsuit edition which I believe is being shot this week in Bali."

"Writing isn't required for this year's spread. It is to be all photography. Anyway, our readers are more than a little interested in the connection between you, the US Open and the new golf equipment company, FiveOnFive."

"Of course they are and well they should be. The golfing story began many years before my unfortunate and unscheduled arrival at this very airport. I quite literally fell from the sky heralded by a lightning bolt of enormous consequence.

Do you know anything about private airplanes?"

"Not really."

"That's fine, though you're missing a big slice of what makes life worth living.

A Piper Cherokee 300 is a fine aircraft though mine was admittedly older than most. It could still haul a pretty good load at a fair speed and that was exactly what I was asking it to do on November 10th, 1994.

Its cargo that day was the final residence of Mr. Leon Greenfeldt. His recently-occupied casket had to make the journey from Carlsbad, California to Beaumont, Texas within 24 hours of his death to serve Jewish tradition. The task was heaped shamelessly on me by a well-meaning but less than thorough friend, Eddie Ray Farrell.

His reasoning was clear. The only way to beat the burial clock was by air and the only way to cut through the formality of government regulations regarding the aerial transportation of a body was to do it privately and quietly. Trading secrets to be kept for forms to be forgotten seemed fair to Eddie Ray. So it made perfect sense to nail Leon's simple pine box shut, toss it in the back of his pickup and show-up at my front door just before sunrise on that Thursday morning.

The story of his friend's death and final request rolled off of his tear stained lips. Like the sucker I am, I bought it, including the part about me removing my Cherokee's rear two rows of seats so we could wedge Leon on board for his swallowesque return to his Texas birth place.

By 8AM we were airborne. Death had come for Leon just six hours earlier. Making the deadline seemed to be a piece of cake which is the way disasters in the making always appear to the fools who create them."

About five seconds after wheels up, Eddie Ray wheezed "How long"?

"It's gonna' be a long day Eddie Ray. We'll be in the air for a good eight hours. Throw in a fuel stop and we're talking nine hours block-to-block. If all goes according to plan, you'll be on the ground in Beaumont sometime around 4 PM.

When's the funeral?"

"When we get there.

No one's coming but me, Leon, of course, and the local Rabbi.

It'd be good if you came too."

The flight had begun in the normal fashion led by a quick call to weather to see how good or bad the day would be. Followed by a casual, pre-flight inspection of the ship and finally sliding the throttle forward to become part of the sky once more.

The report called for clear skies and favorable winds all the way so we would fly VFR *(Visual Flight Rules)* rather than IFR *(Instrument Flight Rules)*. The difference affords the pilot the freedom to fly direct rather than following one of many *Victor Airways* which amble across the continent in odd geometric patterns as they connect electronic milepost to electronic milepost. Many miles and precious minutes are added to each aviator's journey by the IFR process. In the day of the GPS, *Victor Airways* make little sense. Flying VFR grants the right to change altitude, speed and direction as necessary without the approval of an air traffic controller. Milton flew VFR whenever possible. Today it was.

"San Diego departure, Piper 785 Charlie Romeo."

"Piper 785 Charlie Romeo, San Diego."

"Piper 785 Charlie Romeo is east bound at 5,500 climbing to 11,500 enroute to Santa Teresa, New Mexico, five tango six. Request VFR flight following."

"Piper 785 Charlie Romeo squawk 0387 and ident."

"0387 on the squawk for Charlie Romeo."

"Milton, I've gotta' piss."

"There's a milk bottle behind your seat, use it."

"You want me to piss into a plastic milk bottle?"

"Not really but I'd rather you did that than wet your pants and stain my upholstery."

"There goes every illusion I had about the luxury of travel by private aircraft. This is just a little south of primitive."

"Suit yourself but we won't be near a restroom for another three hours."

"Piper 785 Charlie Romeo, radar contact. Proceed under own navigation to five tango six. Report reaching 11,500'."

"Piper 785 Charlie Romeo."

A Cherokee 300 climbs at better than 1,000 feet per minute when lightly loaded and near sea level. With our load and altitude it took almost fifteen minutes to claw our way from 5,500 to 11,500 that day. We'd need every foot of that to fly over the mountains that clogged our route.

"Piper 785 Charlie Romeo. Contact Phoenix Center on 119.75. Good day."

"119.75 for 785 Charlie Romeo. Thanks for your help. Good day sir.

Phoenix Center, Piper 785 Charlie Romeo is with you at 7,500' climbing to 11,500'."

"Roger, 785 Charlie Romeo. Contact me when you reach 11,500'."

"785 Charlie Romeo, WILCO.

Eddie Ray, with the 30 knot wind on our tail, I'm pulling power all the way back to 55%. That'll reduce our fuel flow to 11.5 gallons per hour in cruise rather than the 32 gph that we've been pouring down the cylinders of the Cherokee's way too thirsty Lycoming IO-540 powerplant during our climb.

Early on, Lindberg learned that a very modest increase in the pitch of the prop yielded a nice fuel saving without sacrificing airspeed. Why everyone doesn't fly that way is beyond me.

The 'Lindberg tweak' will save us an additional gallon per hour.

All I have to do is adjust the prop to a little bit less than square.

We're gonna' start hitting some pretty good turbulence soon, so give your seat belt an extra tug."

As the clock moves towards 10AM the earth and the air above it heats up across the desert southwest. The hot air rises producing giant 'chuck holes' along our celestial highway. If we could get up where the big boys fly we'd never feel them. That's the nature of the world's weather, most of it occurs below 18,000 feet.

"Phoenix, Piper 785 Charlie Romeo is at 11,500'."

"Roger 785 Charlie Romeo. Phoenix altimeter is 29.3"

"29.3 on the altimeter."

Angela quickly asked, "Why didn't you just go higher, say 19,000'?"

"Every airplane has a maximum altitude that it can reach called its service ceiling, for the Cherokee 300 its 16,250 feet.

The bumps showed up early on this day, just a short time after we crossed the Arizona border. By the time our shadow shown down on New Mexico things were rocking and rolling pretty good. Eddie Ray was turning green around the edges and looked like he might puke any second.

Sometime after we started talking to Albuquerque the tailwind became a headwind. That's not what the weather service had predicted but that's what happened. It didn't affect our planned fuel stop at Santa Teresa at all though we would arrive thirty minutes later than planned.

We both heard the first loud thump coming from the back of the cabin and we simultaneously wondered if it was Leon beating on his casket?

"Is he trying to get out?"

Thump, thump, thump!

The thumps kept coming and it seemed that each was louder and angrier than the one before.

"Eddie Ray, are you sure that Leon's dead."

"Well he was dead when I nailed his coffin shut. I've got the death certificate to prove it! Maybe he's come back to life. Maybe the bumps jarred him enough to get his heart started again. Maybe he's a freakin' zombie!"

"That's plain stupid Eddie Ray. If he's been dead for seven hours his heart can't start pumping again.

Zombies are only in bad movies and TV shows not in the back of my airplane."

"But if he wasn't really dead and just sorta' passed out then he might be waking up and I imagine he's pretty ticked off."

"Wait a minute, you took him to a funeral home and had him embalmed didn't you?"

"Heck no! He's a Jew and they don't believe in that. The doc at the hospital signed his death certificate and turned his body over to me for burial. The hospital has a Rabbi who came up and performed the Tahara ritual."

"And what exactly is that?"

"Well his body was cleansed and ritually washed, and then Leon was dressed in a simple, white muslin robe called a Tachrichim. The Rabbi recited some special prayers, beseeching God to lift Leon's soul into the Heavens for eternal rest.

Milton, the doc thought he was dead, so did the Rabbi and so did I.

Now he's come back to life somehow."

"That was the bad news, Angela. The good news was that Eddie Ray forgot all about his motion sickness and any thoughts of his losing breakfast were off the table."

Thump, thump, thump, CRACK!

"Eddie Ray what was that crack?"

"I don't know and I don't want to know. It sounded like wood breaking.

Can we get this plane on the ground?

Please!"

"Crawl back and see what's going on."

"No way, not me!"

"If you don't I will and if I do whose gonna' fly this plane, Sissy Boy?

Answer nobody, because I'm the only one here who knows how to fly this airplane. If I go back there and Leon is a zombie and he gets me then you'll have to fight with a blood thirsty zombie all the way to the crash site. That may take a while because I'm putting the plane on autopilot and it won't hit the ground until the fuel runs out in two hours or so.

That'd be an awful way to go."

"OK, OK, I'll crawl back and take a look."

Thump, thump, bang, CRACK!

The distance from the cockpit to the rear cabin is about 24 inches. It took Eddie Ray, the better part of 10 minutes to make the trip. He was mighty scared. I was too for that matter.

"Milton, the woods cracking on top of the casket like somebody's been beating on it with a hammer from the inside and the nails around the top are coming loose and the sides are bowed. The only thing holding the lid down and Leon inside is the two cargo straps."

"Well, check 'em and make darn sure they're good and tight!"

"I did. But I can hear Leon moving around inside that box.

When do we land?"

"The GPS and I think we'll be arriving at Santa Teresa in about twenty minutes. Hold together."

We were already talking to El Paso approach so I gave them a shout to let them know that we had 5T6 in sight and would be landing shortly.

"El Paso, Piper 785 Charlie Romeo will be canceling flight following at this time."

"Piper 785 Charlie Romeo, squawk 1200. Frequency change approved. Good day."

"1200 on the squawk for Piper 785 Charlie Romeo. Thanks for your help El Paso."

Milton tried to sound pilot calm and must have succeeded as they asked him no questions so he told them no lies.

"Is that the airport on our nose?" Eddie Ray whispered.

"It is.

Santa Teresa Unicom, Piper 785 Charlie Romeo is inbound for a full stop landing. We'd appreciate an airport advisory."

"Aircraft calling Santa Teresa, the wind is 90 degrees at 16 gusting to 22 favoring runway 10. No reported traffic in the area. Current altimeter is 27.8."

"Santa Teresa Unicom, 27.8 on the altimeter, no reported traffic.

Santa Teresa area traffic, Piper 785 Charlie Romeo is five miles out on an extended final for runway 10 Santa Teresa.

Santa Teresa Unicom, Piper 785 Charlie Romeo is final for runway 10.

Unicom, we're looking for a quick fuel turnaround. Also if you folks have got a hammer we could borrow we'd appreciate it."

"Piper 785 Charlie Romeo, what kind of hammer do you need?"

"A claw hammer would be best."

"Piper 785 Charlie Romeo, we'll meet you on the ramp with the fuel truck and a hammer."

"Santa Teresa area traffic Piper 785 Charlie Romeo is short final for 10, full stop.

The tires squealed as we touched down and made a quick turnoff to head to the ramp."

"Milton, I'm jumping ship when you slow down."

"No you're not. We don't want to cause a scene do we and attract the attention of the locals? Just be cool for another few minutes."

The fuel truck was right where it was supposed to be. The line boy guided us to a stop and chocked our main gear as we rolled out through the right side cockpit door, Eddie Ray first and me second.

In a moment that seemed like an hour the hammer was in my hand. Slowly I opened the BIG cargo door on the left side of the Cherokee, leaned in and listened to the sound of silence. Total silence, no thumping, no banging and no cracking, just the sound of silence.

Suddenly it all made perfect sense to me. Fear immediately gave way to humor. I laughed so hard that tears rolled down my cheeks.

Eddie Ray yelled from 100 yards away, "What's so dang funny?"

"We are," was the only answer I could muster.

Eddie Ray approached with caution but approached none the less and soon stood next to me at the cabin door. "What changed?"

"Hear anything?"

"No, no I don't. How come? Did you re-kill him?"

"No you idiot. Leon wasn't moving around ever and he wasn't trying to get out of his casket. He was simply being tossed around by the 'bumps" and unlike us and his casket, Leon wasn't wearing a seat belt. So the 'thumps' we heard was Leon banging into his casket. A time or two he hit so hard that he cracked the casket and knocked a nail or two loose."

"Simple as that?"

"Simple as that."

Arrival

Some airports have special departure procedures designed to shield the ears of complaining neighbors. Santa Teresa's have more to do with keeping pilots alive. Ignoring the published procedures risks an up close and personal encounter with one of the nearby brown mountains; all rocks and no trees.

After leaving the field's 4,100' elevation a pilot must gain almost 3,000' before starting his journey. The procedure is pretty simple. Circle and climb to 6,800', cross over the airport before proceeding on course.

It would be tougher for 785 Charlie Romeo today as the weather was deteriorating to the east. An unexpected tropical wave was moving north from the Gulf of Mexico and kicking things up as it did. This was the headwind factory that had bedeviled Eddie Ray and Milton from just west of Albuquerque.

The wind was now blowing 20 knots straight down runway 10 with gusts to 35 knots. It promised to be much more forceful aloft. Given the headwind, Milton worried about having enough fuel to reach Beaumont as he slid the throttle forward to get the big bird moving.

The powerful headwind allowed *wheels up* to come quickly.

Milton knew better than to raise the flaps from the takeoff position just yet. Once he made the turn to circle he would need the lift they provided as the headwind became a tailwind and a headwind once more.

"Eddie Ray, it's going to get pretty bouncy as we climb. Leon's more than likely to start moving around. Stay cool."

"Got it."

Milton decided to stay on the eastern heading as long as he could but a circling departure was an absolute necessity. Almost immediately the mountains filled his windscreen. He rolled into a gentle counter-clockwise turn.

Sweat beads dotted Eddie Ray's forehead. He knew Leon wasn't a zombie but he couldn't shake the *"what if's"*.

"El Paso approach, Piper 785 Charlie Romeo is east bound lifting off from Santa Teresa, five tango six."

"Piper 785 Charlie Romeo, El Paso."

"Piper 785 Charlie Romeo is in route to Beaumont, TX, bravo papa tango. Request VFR flight following."

"Piper 785 Charlie Romeo squawk 0478 and ident."

"0478 on the squawk for 785 Charlie Romeo."

Milton carefully selected the NEXRAD screen on the Cherokee's number two Garmin 430 leaving the number one free for navigation. The weather depictions it provided made flying safer. With it, a careful pilot could easily avoid getting into a weather trap if he understood the age of the picture he was looking at. Most don't, instead they think of NEXRAD as a replacement for onboard radar. It isn't. Instead it displays a collection of ground based radar depictions gathered, collated and transmitted from the NEXRAD system. By the time it reaches an aircraft's panel mounted display, it is twenty minutes old.

The close in depiction's looked great but the long-range picture was scary. A big and ugly weather maker was advancing from the Gulf as predicted and would definitely cross his line of flight before this day became night and he reached BPT unless it stalled which was not out of the question.

"Piper 785 Charlie Romeo radar contact. Proceed under own navigation to bravo papa tango. What altitude are you looking for sir?"

"El Paso, Piper 785 Charlie Romeo is passing through 7,500' looking for 11,500'."

"Piper 785 Charlie Romeo advise upon reaching 11,500'."

"Charlie Romeo, WILCO."

"Milton, you got anything to eat hidden away on this ship?"

"I've got some peanut butter crackers in the outside pocket of my red backpack. If you want 'em they're yours. I bring 'em along to keep me on my diet. Every time I think about eating those things I reconsider.

How's Leon doing?"

"I can hear him sliding around inside his box put he seems pretty comfortable. All things considered."

"By 'all things considered', you mean about him being dead and all?"

"I do."

"El Paso, Piper 785 Charlie Romeo is level at 11,500'."

"785 Charlie Romeo contact departure at 119.725. Good Day sir."

"119.725 for Charlie Romeo. Thanks for your help good day."

Milton carefully dialed in the new frequency and listened for a break in the chatter.

"El Paso departure Piper 785 Charlie Romeo is with you in route to bravo papa tango."

"Roger 785 Charlie Romeo proceed under own navigation."

"785 Charlie Romeo"

"Eddie Ray, the headwind we're hitting is unreal. We may have to make another fuel stop. I'll let you know but right now I'm showing a 40 knot headwind which is 'no bueno por nada'."

The sky was getting dark to the southeast and flashes of lightning were showing up on the MX11 Stormscope at the 200 mile range setting. Milton trusted the Stormscope more than NEXRAD as it measured actual lightning activity at its actual location in real-time. If a storm was firing up a lot of lightning, brave men landed to fly another day.

"Eddie Ray, I'm seeing a lot of lightning and it's all across our flight path to Beaumont. The frontal boundary is long so getting around it is not going to be possible. That's the bad news. The good news is that it has a thin boundary, no more than 10 miles wide, with clear weather on the backside."

"Milton, can we make Beaumont before sundown? I gotta' get Leon in the ground."

"It'll be tight but I think so. My idea is to land and let the storm pass over us before taking off again. It'll be a little dicey as I want us to get as close as we can to it so we don't have to wait long for frontal passage. The 'pucker factor' is liable to go way up.

Are you in?"

"I guess."

They soldiered on for another two hours. The storm now filled the Cherokee's windshield and consumed the crew's every thought.

"Eddie Ray, its time.

We need to land before this storm eats us alive.

Our best bet is La Grange, Texas. The airport I used to land at there was closed years ago and a new one built so I don't know what it's like.

The Cottonwood Inn was right across the road from the old one. They had the second best chickenfried steak in Texas. I sure would like to eat there again. Man it was some kinda' good.

The ***$100 Hamburger Guide to Airports*** shows a pretty long and wide, hard surface runway with fuel and an FBO. There's nothing about food at the field in the ***$100 Hamburger*** restaurant guidebook on my iPad. So I guess we're back to peanut butter crackers."

"Leon's starting to smell something fierce in case you hadn't noticed. I can't eat anything and may not be able to hold what I've got."

"Houston Center, Piper 785 Charlie Romeo, request."

"Piper 785 Charlie Romeo, Houston Center, say your request."

"Houston Center, Piper 785 Charlie Romeo would like to cancel VFR flight following and file IFR direct to 3T5."

"Roger Piper 785 Charlie Romeo, descend to and maintain 6,000'. IFR direct to 3T5 is approved as filed. Contact Austin Approach on 120.875, good day sir."

"Piper 785 Charlie Romeo direct to 3T5, descending to 6,000'. We will contact Austin on 120.875. Thanks for the help, good day sir."

Before calling Austin Approach, Milton dialed in AWOS at La Grange to get the current airport information which included wind speed, wind direction, runway in use, altimeter setting and the code for the current information report which in this case was Kilo.

"Austin approach Piper 785 Charlie Romeo is with you at 10,000' descending to 6,000', landing three tango five with information Kilo."

"785 Charlie Romeo, Austin, what approach would you like?"

"785 Charlie Romeo would like the GPS for 16."

"785 Charlie Romeo is cleared to the Industry VOR for the GPS 16 Approach to three tango five. Report over the Industry VOR."

"785 Charlie Romeo is cleared to the Industry VOR."

Milton continued the descent to 6,000' and pointed the Cherokee towards the Industry VOR. The weather was getting as wild as he feared it might and hoped it wouldn't. The rain pelted the ship with such volume and force that it sounded like they were inside a washing machine. The good news was they couldn't hear Leon who must be beating the heck out of his casket right now.

"Austin, Piper 785 Charlie Romeo is holding at the Industry VOR."

"Roger, 785 Charlie Romeo cleared to Bokke, descend and maintain 2,600'. Report when reaching Bokke."

"Charlie Romeo."

Quicker than Milton would have liked, the GPS indicated he was crossing Bokke. The procedure called for a teardrop entry to the hold followed by a four nautical mile track. 156 degrees back to Bokke then a two minute turn to 336 degrees for the outbound leg of the hold. No sweat!

"Austin, Piper 785 Charlie Romeo is holding at Bokke."

"785 Charlie Romeo we are showing the airport close to minimums. You are cleared to land."

"785 Charlie Romeo is cleared to land.

Eddie Ray, crawl up front and strap in. We're 12 miles away from the runway. Hold on tight we've got a heck of a crosswind to deal with which promises to make this landing a real crowd pleaser.

Help me spot the runway lights. We've got to see them before I descend lower than 250 feet above the runway's threshold elevation. The controller said the airport may be below minimums. So we may have to go around."

Instantly, there was a huge flash followed by a loud explosion and smoke pouring out of the panel. A loss of all panel lights followed.

"Take this flashlight and shine it on the instruments so I can see what we've got.

Darn! We must have taken a lightning strike which knocked out all of our avionics. Grab the hand held radio out of my flight bag and dial in 120.875.

We're still on course and our flight instruments are good. Going around or trying to make it to an alternate in this weather is the last choice I want to make.

We're landing period."

"Milton! I see it, I see the runway. Do you?"

"Yes, I've got it. Thank God.

I'm going to drop the left wing a bit to compensate for the crosswind.

Piece of cake."

"If it's so easy why are we bouncing around like a leaf? You forget how to land this crate?"

"We've got a gusty, crosswind. It's moving us around a little but I'll have no problem staying on the center line."

With that Piper 785 Charlie Romeo came over the fence and reached for the ground. Just as it touched down …

BANG!

"Heck, we blew the left main gear. I was afraid that might happen."

"Why?"

"Well, all the tires were going to be replaced today. They're a little worn. I have the replacements in my hangar. But you showed up with this time critical mission and I decided that the tires would hold up until I got back to Palomar."

"Looks like you were wrong."

"I'm going to taxi slowly to the FBO's hangar. It will probably chew up what's left of the tire. The rain's still coming down hard so I certainly don't want to leave the plane on the taxiway and walk to the office."

"I'm with you."

"Austin approach, Piper 785 Charlie Romeo is on the ground at three tango five. I'd like to cancel IFR at this time."

"Roger 785 Charlie Romeo. Squawk 1200, frequency change approved. Good day sir."

"Austin, 785 Charlie Romeo, thanks for your help.

La Grange area traffic 785 Charlie Romeo is clear the active.

La Grange Unicom. Piper 785 Charlie Romeo."

"785 Charlie Romeo, La Grange."

"La Grange 785 Charlie Romeo blew a tire on landing. Could you open the door to your big hangar and pull us in?"

"785 Charlie Romeo, shut down on the hangar apron. I'll come with the tug to move you in."

"785 Charlie Romeo. Much obliged La Grange. See you in a minute."

"It sure is dark for 2PM."

"Look off to the east. It's already starting to clear."

Everything happened perfectly.

The door went up.

The lights came on.

The tug hooked on and pulled the tired and wet Cherokee inside the huge empty hangar.

The door closed.

We were safe.

Funeral

Tired and running on nothing but adrenaline Eddie Ray and Milton rolled out of the Cherokee.

"Hi, I'm Buck Slithers." The jovial man in the yellow slicker suit stuck out his drenched hand.

"Great to meet you." Milton profoundly meant that for Buck had saved him from a serious drenching.

"Your tire looks like it needs a new one."

"It sure does. Can you slap one on for us?"

"Absolutely, but first, we need to get one. I can have it overnighted from my distributor in Dallas?"

"Darn, we need to get to Beaumont for a funeral today."

"Well you won't get there in this Cherokee. We've got a rental 172 that'll get you there."

"Unfortunately the guest of honor is shoved into the back of the Cherokee. He's got to get there even more than we do."

Buck peeked into the rear of the Cherokee and saw Leon's simple pine box.

"I can't help you with that. The casket's not likely to fit into the 172 or anything else we've got.

Let me go get some tires ordered for you. There's coffee and stale donuts inside. Help yourself."

"Shoot Milton, Leon's dirt nap needs to start today. I promised him."

"I know, I know.

Hey I've got an idea. What if he didn't get buried in Beaumont? Would La Grange work?"

"Beaumont would be perfection. Texas is a requirement. How are we going to pull off a Jewish funeral in La Grange on short notice?"

"I was in the Marine Corps with a guy from La Grange. David Holman. That's right David Holman. He was a Chaplain. Military Chaplains are trained to conduct burials for all faiths because sometimes that's what they have to do.

La Grange is a pretty small place only 5,000 people live here. Buck's gotta' know him."

Slowly they walked into the office picked up a couple of stale donuts and lukewarm coffee.

"Hey Buck, do you know David Holman?"

"Are you talking about David Holman the Methodist minister?"

"I am."

"Heck yes I know him. Everybody around here knows David. He's the pastor at my church. Why do you ask?"

"I just had a hair-brain idea that we could do the funeral here."

"Well, I wouldn't know about that but Pastor Dave will. People never die on a schedule so your emergency planting ain't his first rodeo. No doubt about that.

He's probably at the church right now. I can run you over there if you'd like or we can just call him. It's up to you."

"It'd be great if you could drive us over. I think this is better done face to face."

Off they went.

No place is far away from any other place in La Grange, its compact. Buck shut his trucks engine off at the church three minutes later.

Earlene Merewether, the church secretary greeted them and announced that Reverend Holman was leaving for an important meeting and was running late.

Just then the door to his office flew open as the man that Milton remembered raced through with one arm in a coat sleeve and the other heading in the direction of its twin.

Earlene had spoken the truth; he was in one heck of a rush.

He froze in his tracks as his eyes locked onto Milton's; his face bore the shock of a man who had just seen a ghost.

"Moooz is it you?
Is it really you after all these years?
Let me look at you, stand still?
My goodness you look the same.
Time has been kind to you my friend.
Why are you here, in my office?

Earlene call Edgar and tell him I'll be late and it can't be helped. No, tell him I need to reschedule until next week. Yes do that. I need to have a long visit with Moooz. We have history."

"I need your help Dave."

"What can I do?"

"Let me introduce Eddie Ray Farrell. He and I left Carlsbad, California at 7AM this morning in my airplane. We were in route to Beaumont to bury his friend, Leon Greenfeldt. The storm that just blew through chased us from the air to an unscheduled landing at Buck's place. To make a long story short we can't continue the journey due to a mechanical issue with the airplane."

"So we need to get you boys to Beaumont quickly. Is that right?"

"Well no. It turns out that we are transporting the deceased. He and his casket are still in the back of the plane.

Dave, there is no family and no large funeral planned. His desire was simply to be buried in Texas. Beaumont was his actual birth place so Eddie Ray chose it for his final resting place. However, Leon would have been happy with any location in Texas. Since we are in La Grange we can bury him here."

"Fair enough. So you want me to do the funeral is that it?

"Yes but there is a wrinkle. Leon is a Jew, an Orthodox Jew. He'll need a Jewish burial and hopefully in a Jewish cemetery. Finally the clock is running. We need to get him buried before sundown."

"Moooz you have not changed a bit. You're issues were always interesting. Knowing you, this one isn't surprising. One of Texas' oldest Jewish communities is right here in La Grange. Let me call my dear friend Rabbi Harvey Gollum and see what he says. Give me a few minutes please.

Earlene get Rabbi Gollum on the phone please."

Dave walked into his office and motioned for the others to follow and take a seat.

The desk set rang signaling Earlene's success.

"Harvey, Dave.

How are you this day my friend?

And your family?

Wonderful.

Harv, I've got a tough one that needs your touch.

In the interest of time I'll give you the short version. Later we can fill in the blanks of this very unusual tale.

An old and dear friend of mine has just made an unscheduled landing at the La Grange airport. In the back of his airplane is a deceased Orthodox Jew who must be buried before sundown today. No arrangements have been made at all as they had planned to conduct the service in Beaumont.

Can you help?"

"There is much to do and little time with which to do it. May I call you back in fifteen minutes?"

"Yes, of course. We'll wait for your call."

The long day and the rigors of the trip were wearing on Milton. He was tired and it showed.

"Moooz let's get some coffee while we wait. I think we've got some Weikel's Bakery kolaches in our break room. They drop some fresh ones off every day about this time."

"I haven't had a good kolache since I left central Texas twenty years ago. That sounds really good."

They entered the break room just as the church's part-time music director, Reba Morehead, was leaving.

Fate was weaving quite a tapestry today. Milton's jaw dropped.

"Reba?"

"Milton?"

Dave smiled and said, "Yes Milton its sure enough Reba. How long has it been?"

They both answered.

"How long? Too long."

They came together in an embrace that was much more than a hug.

She spoke first, "Why are you here? How long can you stay? When can we talk? Oh Milton it is so good to see you."

"Reba, yes we must talk. I'll be around until we're talked out. First, I've got to get a burial arranged and I don't have much time to do it."

"I am so sorry for your loss."

"Reba I've had no loss, just doing a favor for a friend. It's kind of a long story. The deceased is a Jew and he must be buried before sundown tonight. We're hoping that Rabbi Gollum can come through for us. If not, Dave will officiate but we need a burial site."

"Is the family particular about the site?"

"There is no family."

Milton watched Reba's green eyes light up and her checks glow. She had an idea. Knowing her as he once did, the idea was probably so far outside the box that most folks wouldn't consider it until they thought about it for a week then they'd agree that she was right. Reba was the queen of brainstorming.

"Reba, what've you got?"

"A great answer if you're open to it."

"I've got a site ready to go right now out on our ranch."

"What? How?"

"Well Dad dug it this morning for a horse that we expect to die in the next week or so. We all love that horse. So Dad dug a proper grave to put her in. It's up on a hill under a tree over-looking one of our stock ponds. It's a perfect place."

Dave asked, "Reba, are you serious?"

"Heck yes. I'll call Daddy and tell him we're coming. He'll be pleased to give the spot to a stranger in need. We've got a lot of land. The loss of a six by four plot won't be noticed."

"Moooz, Texas still allows burials on private land. Pretty much have to or the ranch families would revolt. The tradition of a family cemetery on the home place goes way back. So we can do this.

Give me a minute Harvey's on the phone.

Hey, Rabbi. Where do we stand?

I see. No problem. I totally understand. No, no I can do it. You've done enough already. See you soon.

Well it's decided. Reba it looks like we'll be doing a funeral for a Jewish man in a horse's grave on your ranch this evening.

Moooz I forgot to ask. Is the deceased in a casket or a body bag."

"Casket."

"That's good. So we're ready to go. Let's do this thing.

Buck can you bring the casket in the back of your pickup?"

"No sweat pastor. I'll get him there."

"Ok you do that. Reba how 'bout you head to the ranch and get ready for us."

"I'll meet you guys at the big house. Dave you know the way. Come to think of it so do you Milton."

"Milton why don't you and Eddie Ray stay with me, we've got some paper work to do."

They scattered like a covey of quail. Reba out the front door, Buck out the back and Milton, Eddie Ray and Dave headed for the pastor's office.

"Well now let's see, there is no next of kin so you Eddie Ray are the executor of Leon's estate, correct?"

"Correct."

"You have a power of attorney executed by the deceased?"

"Yes."

"Do you have a copy of his death certificate?"

"Yes."

"I need to copy some information off of each of them. May I see them please?"

"Absolutely, but they're in the plane. I don't have them with me right now."

"OK, just bring them by before you guys leave town so I can burn a copy for my files."

"Glad to pastor."

"All right, I need to fill out a burial certificate. What was Leon's full name?"

"Marcus Leon Greenfeldt."

"Do you know his date of birth?"

"August 23, 1931."

"Do you know his parent's names?"

"Abraham Joshua Greenfeldt and Hannah Ruth Greenfeldt."

"He died yesterday?"

"No. He passed on at 1AM this morning at Cedar Sinai Hospital in Los Angeles, California."

"Perfect! We're good to go. Give me ten minutes to gather my stuff and reacquaint myself with the burial ritual for an Orthodox Jew and we'll head on out.

One more question. Was Leon ever in the service?"

"Yes, he served in the Air Force as the navigator on a B-29. He was a First Lieutenant."

"Sweet, that justifies my officiating. The man is a veteran. I'm still in the reserves so everything is Kosher, so to speak."

Reba greeted everyone at the door. Buck was already inside as was her father, Michael Morehead and her brother Jimmy.

Michael spoke first, "Well everything's ready up on the hill."

There was room enough for everyone in Buck's super fancy King Ranch Edition, crew cab Ford F-250. No one could forget how hard it had rained earlier in the day. Making the trip across the ranch in a four wheel drive vehicle with rear dualies meant they were likely to get where they were going.

The sun was beginning its departure from the sky just as they arrived. Michael, Jimmy, Milton, Eddie Ray and Buck acted as pallbearers Reba made an even number but was disallowed as a woman couldn't be permitted to be a pall bearer at a Jewish funeral, one on each corner and one in the middle would have to do. They followed behind Pastor Dave in reverent silence. This was a man's funeral. His life had ended. They wanted to give him a proper send off. People in central Texas are like that.

Pastor Dave became Rabbi David. He spoke the words that needed to be spoken and preformed the rituals that needed to be performed.

Just as they would have done a hundred years ago the pallbearers lowered the casket slowly into the grave using two ropes that they stretched across it. Slowly the casket found the bottom. As they had been instructed each threw a hand full of dirt into the grave. The ceremony was finished.

The next morning, Eddie Ray rose early to jump on a San Antonio bound Greyhound bus. From there he'd fly commercial back to the coast.

Pastor Holman put the finishing touches on Sunday's sermon and wondered why Eddie Ray hadn't dropped off the papers as he had promised.

Buck picked up the tires for Milton's plane and went to work putting them on the Cherokee.

Michael Morehead, with the help of his backhoe digger, closed the grave he provided for a man he had never met. Then found another for the grave his beloved horse would soon require.

Reba went on a long walk down the short streets that make-up downtown La Grange, the seat of Fayette County government. Milton was by her side. They talked about what was, what might have been and what could still be.

Milton was hanging around La Grange and considering a return.

Fate's tapestry wasn't fully woven around these lives but this chapter like Leon's grave was closed.

Or was it?

Courthouse

The old hotel wasn't much but it would be Milton's home for the next few days. He checked in and asked for a room in the back away from the traffic noise on the square. Sleep comes easily in Central Texas.

Early the next morning, Milton dialed Eddie Ray.

"Eddie Ray. Two questions for you.

First, somebody stuffed one hundred $100 bills into my red back pack I figure it wasn't Leon so I'm guessing it was you."

"Hey Milton, figured I owed you something for all your trouble."

"I can go along with that. $10,000 is way above cost but I'll just say thanks because I can use it."

"You helped me. Now I've helped you. We're even." Eddie Ray sounded anxious to get off the phone.

"Second, if you've got any more cash you're looking to unload I'm considering bringing on an investor for a restaurant I'm planning to open."

"How much?"

"$200,000"

Eddie Ray who normally didn't have two nickels to rub together said simply. "I'll UPS it to you."

"You're gonna' UPS cash?"

"That's right, cash, the long green with the short future. Just remember how you got it and ship $5,000 back to me the same way at the end of each month for sixty months starting now.

That mean's $300,000 coming home to Papa not the $200,000 that ran away from home. I'm not your investor. I'm your banker.

Fair enough?"

"Fair enough."

"Before I let you go. Pastor Dave's after me for Leon's Death Certificate and your Power of Attorney for his estate. Can you get those to him?"

"Sure, sure I said I would and I will. My alarm failed me this morning. By the time I got going the Greyhound was honking. Text me Pastor Dave's address and I'll get copies to him."

"Will do.

Thanks again for the cash. Don't be a stranger.

Bye."

"Later."

Reba dropped by for breakfast and to continue their walk around town.

 "I like that old house on Crockett Street. The old two story with the wide porch that goes all the way around the house.

Do you know the one I'm talking about Reba?"

"Sure I do, Milton. It's one of my favorites. Sad to see it go."

"Go?"

"It's scheduled to be torn down to make way for the McMansion some attorney from Houston wants to build. He does a lot of oil and gas work in the county and wants a place to call home when he's in town. The courthouse is just a block away."

They walked on towards the house on Crockett Street, neither knew why but it was a way to pass time together. Soon they stood in front of it, smiled and wondered.

Reba spoke first, "Why do you want this house, Milton?"

"It always said restaurant to me, Reba; a trip back to Grandma's house kinda' restaurant. I want to live on top and open a restaurant on the bottom."

"Remember this house is fixing to be torn down so stop dreaming about what you can't have."

"Well it'll cost somebody pretty good to tear it down won't it?"

"Yes it will," Reba smiled knowingly. "They've been trying to sell it for $5,000 to anybody willing to move it off the lot."

"You still a realtor?"

"I suppose so. My license is active but I don't do anything with it."

"What if I offer to take $6,000 and have it off their lot in two weeks."

"Milton, I had thought about moving the house out to Daddy's place to open a Bed and Breakfast so I checked on the cost of having it moved. The lowest estimate I came up with was $12,000. How can you get it done for less?"

"I can't. Probably it will cost me $12,000 plus another $2,000 to have it done quickly so $14,000 all in. Take away the $6,000 I'm asking and my cost will be $8,000 not $14,000. I can just handle that."

"You always were crafty. I'll put your offer in this afternoon."

"No, do it now. I want to know now."

"OK, I will but first tell me where you're moving it."

"One step at a time Baby Girl, one step at a time. Make the call."

Reba's long, slender fingers danced across her cell's keypad.

"Jerry? It's Reba. I've got an offer for you on the Crockett Street property."

Jerry Granatti laughed out loud. "What you got?"

"$6,000."

"I'm sure that'll fly Reba. It's more than we're asking."

"No Jerry it isn't. Hear me out.

We're asking your client to pay us $6,000 to take it off his hands. We'll guarantee to have it moved in two weeks and cover all clean-up expenses. The alternative is for your guy to pay $20,000 to have it moved someplace else or more to have it demolished in place."

"Reba, I got you. I'll present the offer. It makes some sense. Can you hold on? I'll call my client's rep. right now and see what he says.

Hold on.

Reba, you still on the line?"

"Yes."

"Good news. You got it!

But we've got to close tomorrow."

Reba smiled as she glanced at Milton. Her phone had been on speaker and he heard every word.

"Let's do it, Reba. Tell Jerry we'll see him at the court house at 10 o'clock tomorrow morning."

"Jerry, can you meet us at ten tomorrow? We'll bring the paperwork you bring the cash. The courthouse is probably the best place to meet."

"I'll be there, Reba, I'll definitely be there."

Jerry smiled as he leaned way back in his chair. The albatross he had been trying to unload for almost a year was soon to be somebody else's problem,

"Great! See 'ya then, Jerry."

"Looks like you're on your way, Milton.

What else can I do to help?"

"Check on two things.

First what would the county lease me a pad for at the new airport and second how much would they take for the old airport."

"You want to open a restaurant at the airport?

That's a get poor quick plan. There can't be more than three airplanes a week that land there."

"I know. Just do your stuff Baby Girl. I've got a whole different plan."

"Well Daddy's on the airport board and the County Commissioner's Court. What if he could get you a 99 year lease for $100 a month?"

"That would be a good start. Could you arrange a sit down with Michael for me?"

"Easy. Come by for dinner tonight. Daddy eats early say six o'clock?"

"I'll be there."

They parted quickly as each had much to do.

Milton punched some numbers into his phone.

"Sam Flaxman?"

"Yes this is Sam. Who's on the line please?"

"Sam its Milton Muzny."

"Moooz. It's been years."

"Far too many years, Sam. How's Mamie?"

"She died. May God rest her soul?"

"How are you?"

"I'm good Milton. Very, very good but you didn't call after all these years to check on my health. What's up?"

"Sam I just bought a house in downtown, La Grange. I need to move it to a spot three miles away and do so within two weeks."

"That's an expensive problem you have."

"La Grange is near Bastrop isn't it?"

"Yes."

"Here's what I can do. I have a truck and a crew heading to Bastrop right now. They were going to start on a house there tomorrow. We have some time on that project so I can send them your way."

"Terrific."

"Tell me about your house."

"Two stories, steep pitch roof, wide porch all the way around, steps front and back. Each floor is roughly a thirty by forty foot rectangle. The frame is oak and cypress."

"Roughly $10,000 on the takedown and move plus $3,000 on the setup. Maybe more, maybe less but about that."

"Can you make me a cash price Sam."

"Do you mean cash as in bills?"

"I do."

"I could come off some, I suppose."

"Let's do it."

"My crew chief will call you tomorrow for directions. His name is Kevin Rodriguez. Irish mother, Spanish father accounts for the name. He's a hot head but he'll get the job done."

"Drinks soon Sam?"

"Very soon Milton. I'm 87 how many more evenings can I have for drinks?"

"Until then Sam."

"Until then Milton."

The airport loaner truck didn't have a real muffler. Arriving unannounced anywhere was not possible. Milton drove the quarter mile from the front gate to the front porch of the Morehead Ranch slowly to keep the noise down to a Panzer-like roar. It didn't help. His hosts stood waving on the front porch as he pulled up.

"Welcome Milton." Michael was a gentleman's gentleman.

"Evening Reba, Michael, Jimmy. Thanks for having me."

They walked inside and headed toward the study which overlooked the lake sized swimming pool. The Morehead's had two things going for them; oil and automobile dealerships. Horses, cattle and land were symbols of their wealth not the source of it.

"So Milton, bourbon?"

"If you had rum I'd rather go that way."

"I have Rhum Agricole Vieux Niesson. Do you know it?"

"Of course, to my taste it is the best rum in the world. Comes from Martinique, doesn't it."

"Yes that's right. It is cane juice rum, which sets it apart from all others. They are made from molasses."

"That'll work, Michael, if you don't mind mixing it with Coke and adding a lime."

"How much lime?"

"Two wedges would be about right."

"You've described the perfect Cuba Libre.

So what's this Reba tells me about you opening a restaurant at the airport?"

"That's exactly what I want to do."

"Frankly, it sounds crazy.

The restaurants downtown are struggling."

"They should. All they offer is food. Some of it is good and some of it is bad but at the end of the day, they're just slinging hash."

"You have a way with words.

But tell me; what's different about a restaurant at the airport, other than having fewer prospective customers passing by?"

"Successful restaurants today aren't about food, they're about entertainment.

Theme restaurants have been the rage for the past two decades. No one wants to just eat fried shrimp. They want to be immersed in a seafaring experience. They want to feel that they've taken on a mini-vacation not merely gone out for dinner.

That's a fact."

"So you think the airport provides the theme?"

"No, no I don't.

I think it provides an unbeatable venue for an aviation themed restaurant.

No matter how many dead fish you mount on the wall of a restaurant on the town square you'll never have shrimp boats steam passed the front window, dump trucks maybe but no shrimp boats."

"The airport venue is the perfect place for magic to happen. For the price of a meal you become part of the flying community. It's a dining adventure."

"Milton, you are a silver tongued Oreo.

But don't many restaurants located at country airports like ours fail, change hands and fail again. Isn't that because not enough people fly anymore and they wind up with fewer and fewer customers?"

"That's true but I'm not trying to succeed by feeding pilots. My success will rest on luring in the town's people and highway travelers. It isn't about emptying the wallets of airport bums.

Please hear me out.

Airshows are the number one *'fair'* category event across America. The crowds get larger each year not smaller. People come to see others fly and each secretly dreams that one day they might as well. The problem isn't a lack of interest in the venue. The problem is identifying and connecting with the right market. I'm counting on transient pilots to provide a free show."

"That's interesting.

What kind of food will you serve?"

"The name of the restaurant says it all, **The Chickenfried Café**."

"Chickenfried steak is a good choice. What else?"

"Nothing else."

"One item on the menu?

I've never seen that done before."

"It gets worse, Michael. We'll serve only one meal a day, five days a week, closed Sundays and Mondays."

"That's a stretch son.

Another Cuba Libre?"

"Please.

Our menus, billboards and website will stress three issues.

1. The '**Second Best Chickenfried Steak in Texas'**.
2. **No tipping**. We pay our staff so you don't have too.
3. **FREE Airshow** daily.

The ambiance will be upscale wholesome. White table clothes, quality but not luxurious flatware, glasses and pottery.

We'll put on an airshow everyday – no charge!

Area pilots flying in will eat for **FREE**, if they sit at our **Skygod's Table**.

A **FREE** ground school will be taught every Wednesday afternoon for folks interested in becoming pilots. If they hang in and finish the six weeks long course and pass the FAA's written examination their first flying lesson will be on us."

"Are you on a crusade to save aviation or are you trying to build a successful restaurant?"

"Neither, I intend to build a **CHAIN** of financially successful restaurants. Doing just one would not be interesting to me or you I suspect."

"Are you looking for a partner?"

"No, a mentor.

I will be working with publically owned airports. I don't know much about how that world operates. You do.

La Grange for example, I need a pad near the office with plenty of airplane tiedowns on the apron side of the fence and a large parking lot for cars on the other side.

Because I will be committing a lot of money to erect a restaurant at the airport, I need to know that I can count on keeping it there for many years and that I can transfer the lease if the mood strikes me. A ninety nine year term at $99 a month seems right.

I want the county to provide the pad and the slab. My business will enhance the airport by bringing customers and revenue for the other airport tenants plus increased tourism to the downtown area.

Some promotion will be required to launch and sustain my project. It will be the obligation of Fayette County to provide two billboards on the highway leading to the airport, one mile away from it in either direction plus two smaller 'turn here' signs near the entrance of the airport.

Naturally the restaurant must be prominently included in all airport advertising.

One more thing, Fayette County must cover the first $200,000 of my construction costs. In return, I will deed the property back to the county upon the termination of my 99 year lease.

I want all of that and whatever else you can bundle in from Fayette County and your advice and leadership on how to the get the same or better deal from every future airport that is selected to host a **Chickenfried Café**."

"You're asking a lot."

"I'm bringing more,"

"I'll help if Reba runs your books and Jimmy manages one of the restaurants. Preferably the one that's farthest away from here. He drives me crazy hanging around the ranch.

You buy your beef from me and never argue about the price."

"Shake on it?"

"Let's do this thing."

"Dinner's ready Daddy grab Milton and head for the upstairs dining room." Reba's voice sounded especially good after two Cuba Libres.

"Moooz, let's take the elevator, my leg hurts."

The paneling opened in an unexpected place to reveal a room size people lifter.

"Sometimes we have several people over and one of those sardine sized boxes just wouldn't do the trick."

Michael pressed the button marked four and off they went.

The top floor of the Morehead home was given over to a huge terrace, a small dining room and a magnificent view which had been customized by bulldozers carefully rearranging the landscape to suit Michael's constantly changing imagination. This year's pecan grove was next year's Japanese koi pond complete with weeping willows.

"Reba, you do clean-up particularly well. The only word that comes to mind is stunning!"

She was still the most beautiful woman in this part of Texas, perhaps the most beautiful woman anywhere.

"Well Milton, a little bird told me that you like chickenfried steak. So guess what we're having for dinner?"

"I am deeply flattered."

"Don't be. We're having lobster!" Reba laughed loudly at her own joke.

Dinner was good, the conversation polite and predictable. At 8:30 precisely, Milton announced that he had to leave.

"Late date?" Reba's tone gave her away. She was not happy that he was evening so early.

"Reba, I'm sorry but I've got a lot to do before our closing tomorrow."

"I understand. I'll meet you at the courthouse."

The truck fired up and startled every living thing for three miles.

He wheeled passed Tom Joiner's house on the way back to the hotel. Hopefully the best architect in Central Texas would be around. Milton had phoned earlier in the day to explain what he was thinking about doing. Tom was a lifelong La Grange resident and welcomed the idea of a new restaurant in his town.

The lights were on, so Milton parked, walked to the front door of a really well done Georgian house and pressed the doorbell.

"Tom? Milton Muzny."

"Well now, Mr. Muzny I am indeed pleased to meet you. Come inside and tell me all about your project."

Milton laid all of his cards on the table. Tom agreed that the Crocket Street house projected the ambiance that Milton wanted but he disagreed with trying to turn it into a restaurant.

"The cost of modifying it will be great and the outcome will be slight. You will be disappointed, I assure you. I propose that we simply design the perfect new structure following the style of the Crocket Street house. It will suit your purpose better while projecting the comfortable Grandma's House fantasy you want to create. I'll do either but you'll be happier with new build."

"What about costs?"

"They favor new build. At least twice a year I get involved in renovating a historic structure. It is **ALWAYS** more expensive than starting fresh and the results are generally a pile of compromises. Never does it end-up being what the owners thought they wanted."

"What would it cost to build what I'm looking for and how long would it take?"

"If you have the land and the permits, it could be done in sixty days. Currently construction cost for the commercial structure we are discussing will come in at $100 a square foot give or take. I'd need at least three weeks to get some plans together. We could start as soon as you approve them."

"I appreciate everything your saying but I'm already committed to the renovation. Do you think you can dig up a set of plans for the existing structure?"

"Probably not but it doesn't much matter. We can figure it out."

"Great, can we get together tomorrow afternoon to get things moving. I'll have the keys by then so we can get inside to have a look around and plan the renovation."

They said goodnight. Milton walked to his room in the hotel on the square, unlocked his door and fell asleep with his boots on. Long days are good days.

Morning came early but it didn't matter; the court house was right across the street. About 9AM he dressed, picked up a heavy UPS package from Eddie Ray at the front desk, shoved its contents into his duffle bag and wandered to the mom and pop café next door for breakfast.

Positioned near the window he could see Reba arrive and watch her sweat out his arrival. She'd be early and he'd be late.

Soon, his phone alarm buzzed signaling appointment time. No Reba. He began to wonder if she was coming. He paid the check and walked out front. Reba's fire engine red 1976 Cadillac Eldorado convertible slid to a stop in the no-parking space just in front of the Courthouse.

"I don't think Sheriff Jim will give me a ticket, do you?"

Milton shook his head, "No I expect not."

There were two men walking up the steps to the courthouse just across the street from them. Milton guessed that they were the seller and his agent.

"Do you know Jerry?" Reba purred.

"Never laid eyes on him."

"He's the one on the left. I don't know the other guy."

"Let's go get introduced. I'm betting he's the owner.

By the way, I tried only two cases in my life, both in this courthouse."

"Milton, I knew you went to law school but I didn't remember you ever practicing."

"We hadn't met yet. After the first year of law school, I knew that I didn't want to be a lawyer. During that year you learn what a lawyer does. The next two years are devoted to how he does it. The life of a lawyer is given over to disagreement and contention. A lawyer argues. Accepting conflict as the foundation of life is contrary to my nature. The two cases I tried in this building confirmed by feelings about litigation. I then looked for any area of law that wasn't based on struggle. There aren't any. Life is not a zero sum game and I didn't want to live pretending that it was.

The computer business was my plan B. It is the exact opposite. People worked together towards a common goal that enriched everyone.

Reba smiled but said nothing. She had just learned that Milton was who she thought he was; a man who loved life, encouraged his friends and cared for strangers. He was a builder not a battler.

"Hi Reba, this is Mac McFarland the owner of Crockett Street."

"Mr. McFarland, what a pleasure to meet you at last. We're all excited to see the new home you intend to build on the Crockett Street lot."

"Me too, if the house matches the plans Tom Joiner drew I'll be very happy."

"Let me introduce you both to Mr. Milton Muzny."

They spoke almost in unison and shook hands as they were supposed to, "Pleasure to meet you Mr. Muzny."

Reba brought everybody back to their purpose, "I have all of the paperwork. We just need some signatures and some cash. Then I'll get it filed and we'll be done."

Jerry spoke quickly, "Reba, there's an issue with the cash."

"Don't worry about it Jerry. I'm certain Mr. McFarland's check is good."

"I wish it were that simple. Mr. McFarland didn't understand that he was to pay Mr. Muzny to take title to the house until we reviewed the deal at breakfast this morning."

McFarland jumped in, "No way am I paying anybody to take the house. I planned to sell it cheap and I might even have agreed to give it away but there is no way that I'm paying somebody to take it."

Milton smiled but held back his laughter, "So we're done here?"

"No, I want to do a deal but a fair one." McFarland was near yelling now.

"Well I thought it was a good deal but now I'm not so sure. It will cost you $12,000 or so to have the house moved plus you need a lot to put it on so you'd be in for $20,000 at least if you went that way. Then what? Do you try to sell it? Do you rent it? What? Or I suppose you could have it demolished but that would likely cost even more and take much longer, stretching the start date on your new home.

I agree with you though, paying me $6,000 is a bad deal.

I won't do it for less than $12,000. I was being two generous." Now Milton did laugh as he turned to leave.

"You seriously expect me to do that?"

"No, no I don't. I expect that your next call will be to a demolition company."

"You're wrong you greedy bastard. I intend to move the house to the airport and open my own damn restaurant. Tom Joiner called me last night and let me know that he had pretty much talked you out of doing the conversion and advised me that I should. So I'm going to."

"Good luck with that Mac."

"It's a big world with plenty of room for all of us, lots of airports and lots of houses to be moved. Good luck with your project." Milton continued to laugh so hard that he could no longer speak.

"What's so damn funny?"

Reba answered as Milton couldn't and Jerry was speechless, "Well Mr. McFarland. You had a chance to have your lot cleared and be ready for construction in just two weeks. Now you're going to spend a half million dollars or so to open a business that you don't know anything about and don't possibly have the time to run. The guy who wins in this deal is the architect, Tom Joiner, who you're going to pay twice, once to build you a house and again to build you a restaurant. Mac, you're cutting off your nose to spite your face and that's beyond funny it's hilarious."

Mac turned beet red and looked like he would explode. Remembering who Reba's father was and the power he swung, Mac bit his tongue and simply said goodbye.

Reba and Milton jumped into her car and headed out.

She spoke first, "Milton, what are you going to do?"

"First I'll pass Mac McFarland's number along to Sam Flaxman."

"Why would you do that?"

"Sam will appreciate the lead and I want Mac to get used to wearing out his checkbook on this one. Sam and all other building movers get their money upfront. I figure Mac will think about the $6,000 check he could have written to me this morning while he's writing a $14,000 check to Sam this evening. When he gets to the line on Sam's form that asks for the 'Move To' address he'll choke over all the work he needs to do to get permission from the County Commissioner's Court and the Airport Board to build and operate a restaurant at the airport."

"So you want to rub it in?"

"I do."

"Daddy made some phone calls last night to his cronies to get the things you talked with him about. That's the good news. The bad news is that I know Mac may be better wired than Daddy in some places."

"Well Reba we'll just have to hide and watch. My bet is I missed my chance. Maybe not, but that's what it looks like."

"Then I missed my chance too Milton."

"Maybe not, but for now I need to get back to California to check on a few things. Can you drop me at the airport?

"OK." That's all she could say as the tears started to trickle down her cheeks.

"It's not as bad as that Baby Girl. I'll be back."

"That's what you said, all those years ago."

He laughed, "Well see, I said I'd come back and here I am."

They said goodbye and he walked into the airport office.

Buck was ready with his fuel and tire bill. Milton looked it over and said. "Looks fair to me Buck, can you run it on my card or do you need cash?"

"The card will be fine Milton."

"I need to spend a few minutes to work on a flight plan back to Palomar."

"Are you going now?"

"Probably this evening. The winds and the thermals will have gone to bed by then. It should make for an easy ride with minimal headwind."

"Makes sense to me.

Milton, any truth to the rumor that you might open a restaurant at this airport?"

"Well I'm considering it but there are some hurdles I need to jump."

"I can help you with that."

"How?"

"Easy.

My contract which has ten years to run gives me first right of refusal on any new business coming in here and it restricts the number of each type to just one. There can be only one FBO, that's me, and only one restaurant, I hope that's you."

"You made my day. Let's do this thing."

He dialed Reba.

"What's up, Milton?"

"I'm back, can you pick me up at the airport?"

"I can just work you in." Reba did a fast u-turn and floored her powerful red car.

Renovation

Milton mashed the buttons on his phone for Sam Flaxman, "Sam, this is Milton. I have to cancel the move I scheduled. Turns out I don't own the building."

"I know."

"How do you know?"

"Well I had Southern Title Company do a quick run-up on the address. Regardless of what my customers tell me I always get independent confirmation that they own what they think they own so I don't get sued or arrested for stealing the rightful owner's house."

"Well Mac McFarland, the owner, backed out of our deal this morning. I'm calling to give you his name and number. Maybe you can work out a deal with him."

"I don't know who he is but I do know that he doesn't own the property on Crockett Street. The State of Texas did. They condemned it three years ago over a radon issue. It's an easy fix but the owner decided not to do anything about it so the state moved in. I figured you didn't know about it so I bought the property this morning for a buck. I'll sell it to you for two dollars if you hire me to move it."

"**WOW!** That is amazing news. You saved my bacon."

"I figured you'd be pleased."

"Pleased? I've never felt this good in my life. Have your guys pick-up my house and move it to the La Grange airport."

"They're scheduled to start at 4PM today. By the way, they have all of the papers on this deal with them. Your title to the house and our contract. Your end is to hand over $14,002 in cash. I figure that amount squares us."

"Sam, you really bailed me out."

"Good afternoon Milton. I've got to go now."

"Busy?"

"No, it's time for my nap. I'm a seriously old guy."

"Later Sam."

"Buck, the house I'm going to turn into a restaurant will be here in a week or so. Can we get the airport board to move that fast?"

"Probably not but they don't need to do anything. I have the right to throw up a building anywhere on the airport I want too with the prior permission of the airport manager.

Did you know that I'm also the airport manager?"

"No I didn't realize that you had that much rank and horsepower."

"What about a building permit?"

"That's on you but it should be easy. What you're really going to need quickly is a permit to hook up to the city water and sewer. That can sometimes be a problem."

"I'll get to work on it."

Just then the tires of Reba's red Caddy screeched to a stop announcing her arrival."

"Milton, what's up?"

"So much Baby Girl so much, I'll fill you in as we head towards town."

"Thanks Buck. Thanks so much."

"You're welcome neighbor."

"Reba, we need to talk. Things are piling up and moving fast. I need your help bad."

"You've got it."

"I want to propose ………………"

She cut him off right there and laughingly asked, "So there's a ring involved?"

"No Reba this is a business proposal. I want you to come to work with me as the **Chickenfried Café's** business manager."

"OK, if I call all the shots, no if I don't."

"It's a yes when it comes to business. I do marketing and strategy. The rest is yours."

"Including cash management?"

"Especially cash management, I have $200,000 all in cash in this duffle bag. Please take it and do the best you can to get us up and running."

"Step one is to take it to Daddy's bank and open an account. Have you incorporated the **Chickenfried Café**?"

"That's your job not mine."

"You haven't done anything have you?"

"I hired you."

"What do you need me to do now?"

"I need you to tie-up all of the loose ends."

"How much time do we have?"

"The Crockett Street property will be here next week at the latest. By then, we need to have a pad with a slab on it and all the required permits.

For now, we've got to get over to Crockett Street for the fireworks show.

It should be fun to watch Mac explode at the news. I own his house and the lot he thought he was going to build on is the closest thing to Love Canal La Grange has ever seen. It's unbuildable – for now plus I own it!

Life is good!"

"You've got a dark side. I kinda' like it. Let's get on over there."

Just as they pulled up Sam's moving crew arrived. Milton traded $14,002 in cash for the papers as promised which let them get right to work.

Within a few minutes Jerry and Mac showed up. Jerry walked at a fast pace trying to keep up with Mac who rode his showy Segway.

Mac leaned the thing against a tree and yelled at Milton, "What the hell is going on here?"

Milton just smiled and said, "Oh these guys are moving my house."

"I'll have the Sheriff arrest your dumb ass if you don't get off my property immediately."

"Actually they're mine not yours, the house and the lot."

"Yours? That's a load of crap, I didn't sell them to you remember?"

"That's true and it's good you didn't because you never owned them. Your boy Jerry didn't do a good job of checking out the title on this property before you 'closed'. The guy who sold it to you didn't own it.

Mac, I have no interest whatsoever in the lot just the house. I would be pleased to sell you the lot."

"You're offering to sell me a lot I already own and you're prepared to steal the house that sits on it that I also own?"

Milton smiled more broadly than ever, "Jerry did you run a title search on this property before Mac closed and did you buy a title policy or did you simply decide to save your client a few bucks on something you felt he didn't need?"

Jerry was seven shades of yellow and white with a little pea soup green mixed in. His head sunk as he spoke, "No I didn't call for a title search and no, I didn't buy a title policy."

Mac shifted his anger from Milton to Jerry, "You idiot. You complete idiot. I'll have your license over this one."

Jerry moaned as Milton spoke, "Now Mac, think for a minute. If you sue 'ole Jerry here, word will get out about what happened and you'll ruin your reputation as a lawyer people can rely on to protect their property interest. Gosh, if you can't even look out for yourself…………

Well you get my point."

Mac certainly got the point. He hated that Milton got the better of him. But he decided to go along to get along and take his chances of settling the score at a later date. Revenge is a dish best served cold.

"How much do you want for the lot, Milton?"

"What do you think would be a fair price, Mac?

Before you speak I have to disclose that the lot has a radon issue."

"A radon issue, what the heck is radon?"

"Radon is a radioactive gas that comes from the natural breakdown of uranium deep within the earth's crust. It causes lung cancer."

"Holy shit why would I want to buy this lot if living here could kill me?"

"Because there are people you can hire who can fix the problem at a reasonable cost.

If you want to pursue it let me know. If not I'll have Reba list it."

"Shit, I need some time."

"Mac, you've got 24 hours that's the best I can do. Heck I might want to build a townhouse here for myself."

"Milton, I'm really angry right now. I'll be in touch when I cool down."

When the fireworks started Reba quietly wandered off to the courthouse. She filed the deed in Milton's name, pulled a building permit for the foundation the Crockett Street house would need at the airport and applied for a water and sewer permit. The building permit was an immediate rubber stamp item as it was only a foundation she was filing for; the sewer and water connections would take a week. They needed to be reviewed by the La Grange Public Works Manager, Charles Reed Brown.

Sam's crew chief, Kevin Rodriguez didn't even bother listening to the argument on the driveway. He just got busy. Moving a house isn't easy but it can be done on schedule by doggedly following a set of steps. The first is to have the crew set jacks between the house and the ground below it. This old house rested on blocks placed at its corners and a couple of strategic points near its center.

Part of the crew set the jacks while others disconnected the water lines, sewer lines, gas lines, phone lines and electrical connections. Kevin toured the house to find things that could be removed.

Moving houses is all about weight. If there was any furniture left in the house Kevin wanted it gone.

"What about the bathrooms and the kitchen?" Kevin yelled at Milton.

"Can I gut them?"

Milton thought quickly, "Yeah go for it."

This was really happening and Milton hadn't a clue about how to do it. He needed an architect. There was only one in town and there was no way Milton would use Tom Joiner the rat.

Then it hit him – free student labor. He'd call on the head of the architecture school at Texas A&M and see if he had any stars who would be available to intern on his classic home to restaurant renovation.

"Reba, where you been?"

"I've been taking care of business while you were having fun getting even with Mac. What's up?"

"I just had a nuclear idea about using a couple of interns from A&M to design and supervise this renovation. You know anybody at the college of architecture?"

"Yeah, the department head chased after me for a while. I could give him a call but it'll cost you."

"I'll pay any price."

"In that case, I'll get busy mashing buttons."

With that Reba punched Steve Sadler's number into her cell phone.

"Hey Steve, Reba."

"Reba, Oh My God, how good to hear your voice. To what do I owe my good fortune?"

"I need a favor."

"Name it."

"Steve, there's a beautiful old house on Crockett Street in La Grange. It was built in the early 1900's in the style of the day. You know, two stories with a lot of gingerbread for decoration and a wide roofed porch circling the entire first floor. It is to be moved to a new location and renovated into a restaurant while retaining all of its original character and ambiance. The budget is modest so I'm hoping to grab a couple of your best and brightest to head up the design and supervision of this project as interns."

"Done!

It is amazing that you called at just this moment. This is the time of year that we hook up our students with projects. The guy running a project that I had assigned to my two brightest kids just phoned to say his project had lost funding. If you can use two, you've got 'em. As a matter of fact I'll fly them over tomorrow afternoon. Can you pick us up at the airport?"

"Glad to, I look forward to seeing you and meeting the crew."

"See you around three. Bye for now."

Milton insisted on driving Reba out to the airport to pick up Steve and the interns.

"Why Milton are you jealous of my old flame?"

"Maybe."

Right on schedule a maroon and black Cirrus SR22 touched down at 3T5. The tail number was a dead giveaway that an Aggie was at the controls, 1939AM. The numbers signified the year TAMU last won the National Championship for college football. The letters are overkill. Aggies are like that.

"Steve, I didn't remember that you were a pilot."

"I wasn't but the design of the Cirrus and the size of Texas makes it hard to say no to private aviation. My role causes me to travel around the state quite a bit. Cirrus solved my major objections to general aviation and flying my own plane; safety, comfort and mission control.

The full aircraft parachute solves the safety issue for me. The Lexus like interior and the air conditioning fix the comfort problem and a panel full of 21st century avionics fixes my mission control concern.

I enter my flight plan into the Garmin 1000 and turn the flying over to the autopilot while I monitor the traffic, weather, terrain, engine performance and flight profile.

It truly is a magic carpet."

"Steve this is my friend Milton Muzny. He is also a pilot. The project I'm involved with is actually his. You'll be pleased to know that the house we're moving and the restaurant it is to become will rest right over there next to the FBO on the big ramp."

"Hi Milton. Tell me about your restaurant concept."

"The name and location says it all. The **Chickenfried Café** will combine the comfort of a trip to Grandma's house with the excitement of aviation. We'll serve one meal a day, lunch. It includes a **FREE** airshow and hopefully a stream of flyin pilots to delight the highway travelers and town folk who are the intended customer base."

"Milton, I've made more than a few $100 Hamburger flights. Man I look forward to your opening. This is such a short flight from Easterwood field.

Let's grab our equipment and have a look at the house we're going to repurpose.

First let me introduce you to your interns and project managers, Jenny Clayton and Madison Kessler."

"Welcome aboard. I've got a lot riding on you. Don't let me down." Milton spoke in his most serious tone.

"We won't sir." They spoke in unison.

"So Steve what does all of this equipment do?"

"Simply put it measures every detail of the property while it video tapes and makes a thermal image of it. When we get back to the shop, Jenny and Madison can construct a 3D model of the building in its current state. The thermal image shows us the buildings 'bones' so we'll know what we can remove and what we have to reinforce. The team will then make an electronic model of the restaurant and get your approval of their concept. Next they'll reduce the model to a set of plans and a material list to budget the project and once again get your approval before pulling final permits, ordering materials, hiring subcontractors and supervising construction.

Piece of cake."

They rode to the house in Buck's truck. It was the only thing around big enough to carry everyone plus the equipment. By the time they arrived at the house Kevin and his crew were ready to start the lift that would allow them to slip the big steel I-beams of their giant house moving trailer into position. The lift would take three days to accomplish. It is a game of inches. Twelve screw jacks were positioned under the floor beams of the house. In a cross pattern one was twisted slightly to raise the house no more than ½" then the one diagonally across from it was raised to the same level as measured by laser levers. Then another jack was selected and raised before being followed by its opposite and so it would go for the next three days. All of the utility connections had been removed and thought was being given to the problem of the porches. Could they remain in place for the move?

Leaving them on would mean risking breaking them off if they bounced around too much during the road trip phase of the relocation. Removing them meant taking off the entire porch structure; porch, pillars and roof. Hopefully the neophyte design team would have the answer.

Madison flew out of the truck almost before it stopped and began setting up the equipment for the outside shots. Professor Sadler headed inside to see what they had.

"Milton, I like the feel of the place."

"Me too. I've never been in it before."

"We've got a living room, kitchen, washroom, dining room, bedroom, bathroom room and the stairwell to the second floor. I like it. Let's head upstairs."

"As big as this lot is, there would have been a stable and an out-building or two." Milton opined.

"I counted three bedrooms, a sewing room and one bathroom upstairs. That's good as it indicates there hasn't been much remodeling done since it was originally built. Remodelers typically hurt the structure and cover up their mistakes with wallpaper."

"Ooops! Termites!" Jenny shrieked.

"That's not good. How bad is it?" Reba wondered out loud.

"Well, there are a lot of them, as in thousands."

"OK we'll get an exterminator to come over here and kill them and then we can see how much of this house they had for dinner. Hopefully it's all in an area that was going to be ripped out anyway. Let's be optimistic!" Reba's voice was calm and reassuring.

Kevin Rodriguez heard the scream and came inside quickly.

"What's up?"

"Termites."

"Where?"

"The upstairs bathroom." Jenny was afraid her project was about to be shut down before it started.

"That's typical in these old houses. The cast iron pipes they used, rust out and leak over time and soak the lumber that supports the plumbing stack. Termites are attracted to moist timber. We already spotted them under the kitchen and downstairs bathroom. The fix is pretty simple. We'll inside brace the house before the move. The builders will replace the rotten wood on the other end. First though it's important to kill the bugs so we don't give them a free ride to their new home."

"Kevin, I just spoke with an exterminator. He's on his way over now. It is possible that he may have to tent the place." Reba spoke softly hoping to reassure the team.

"Reba, if they tent this place that adds one to two weeks to our schedule which is more time than we have to wait around. We'd have to move on and get back to you later. My strong suggestion is that you find a guy who's big on shooting bug juice and weak on circus tents."

Reba simply replied, "Gotcha'."

Steve jumped in and said, "Look, there is little to be gained by tenting the place now. We can do that at the new site if we need to. Our thermal imaging study will tell us everything we need to know about the true structural condition of the building and where we need to shore it up during the rebuild. I agree with Kevin. Flood the place with bug juice and move on."

Milton was curious but didn't want to stick his nose too deep into Reba's new found job, "When will you have the 3D model of the existing structure complete with the damage profile, Steve?"

"Two days. No more."

Jenny and Madison breathed heavy knowing that to make the two day deadline Professor Sadler had just laid out there would be no time for sleeping or eating and just enough for potty breaks.

Madison spoke first "Professor Sadler, we've completed the data capture. Will we be heading back soon so we can get started?"

"Madison can't you and Jenny transmit the files and get the process started now?"

"We already have Professor. It is our belief that we don't have much time to massage the data and build the model if we are to meet your deadline."

Sadler laughed, "You're right. I did light a short fuse for you didn't I?"

"Yes Sir. So can we leave?"

"Reba, they're right we gotta' get moving can you get us back to the airport?"

"Milton you coming?" she smiled slyly.

"No Baby Girl. I'm needed here for now.
Good to meet you Steve.
Welcome aboard, Jenny, Madison."

Reba loaded the crew, gave Milton a quick peck on his lips which surprised him and headed off towards the 'port in Buck's truck.

"Kevin, are these bugs a problem?"

"No. I've seen much more damage then you have. We'll just brace a little bit more than usual. No sweat, my friend, no sweat."

Two days later Milton with Reba onboard pointed his Cherokee towards College Station's Easterwood Field. Jenny picked them up. She had a big smile on her face which made them happy and let them know that she wasn't much of a poker player. If she was happy or sad her face told the tale.

The presentation was set up in a small amphitheater normally used to teach 3D modeling. The lights dimmed and the presentation began. Jenny and Madison stepped forward and began to talk as the projections of the Crockett Street house appeared on the screen looking more as it might appear in a photograph rather than a digital rendering. They circled the house and then flew above it to look down at the roof.

Milton couldn't help but comment, "Very cool!"

"You haven't seen anything yet," was Jenny's reply.

As she spoke the exterior planks of the house flew away to reveal the studs, plumbing and electrical. All looked as it might have if you were standing inside the house making a daily inspection as it was built almost 100 years ago. Then they saw the termite damage right where Kevin had suggested it would be. It looked bad to Reba and worse to Milton.

Madison spoke, "I know what you're thinking but don't worry. Fixing this will be easy. It turns out that all of the damaged areas would have been ripped out during the remodel anyway. No loss no extra cost. God is good!"

The door opened, the lights came up, Steve entered and said, "This 'ole house is in darn good shape. It was never remodeled and was properly built. The kids have already started to do the plans for the remodel. They're not finished mind you but would you like to see what we're thinking?"

Jenny and Madison gasped in unison revealing themselves to be very new architects. Naturally they wanted to finish the entire workup before letting the client in on their concept. Steve knew better. Bringing a client in early made the project a collaboration of the designer and the owner. When they reached the final stage everyone was in agreement and no one would have to be told and sold. Experience is the best teacher but that takes time and youth is impatient.

Madison began, "Our biggest design issue is the outside *'airplane watching'* deck. The main dining room is on the first floor. It also must have a view of the runway and the airport activity. The deck blocks its view. A solution can be reached by lowering the deck or raising the building or a little bit of both. Our thought is to introduce a semi-basement with a depth of approximately five feet and a ceiling height of ten feet. That means the steps to the front and back entrances will be five feet high. Easy to do.

We see the kitchen on the north end of the basement with a 15,000 gallon cistern on the south end, between them will be a storage area including the refrigerators, pantries and batteries.

The deck will be covered by a fully retractable awning of broad stripped green and white canvas similar to the one on the Café Du Monde in New Orleans if you're familiar with it. The view from the tables in the first floor dining room will be uninterrupted by the deck or its covering as it will be well above either."

Reba was intrigued, "How will the food get from the kitchen to the dining areas?"

"Great question, to begin with there are four dining areas including the roof top deck which is also covered by retractable green and white canvas. The kitchen is partially below grade as is the airside deck.

'Dumb waiters' which are merely small elevators will move food to the dining rooms on the first and second floors and the roof. A conveyor will do the same for the airside deck."

"Excellent!" Milton beamed as he spoke. "That's exactly what I want. The kitchen should be totally removed from the diners view and disconnected from his dining experience."

"For the moment we've stopped work not knowing enough about your vision for this restaurant. Can you fill us in?"

"Certainly, nothing I'd rather do.

The concept is built on a unique menu and superb presentation.

Our service will be divided into three courses. We start with a salad presentation which includes dinner rolls, followed by an entre of chickenfried steak, mashed potatoes and cream gravy on the side and green beans. A slice of pecan pie completes the meal.

The **Chickenfried Café** is a high value, upscale restaurant. Only one meal is served each day. The setting includes antique styled wooden four-top tables, chairs with comfortably padded leather seats, pressed white table clothes and napkins. The waiters are smartly uniformed. The service is attentive yet quiet. Conversation between server and diner is minimal as there is no menu and the order is placed and paid for before the guests enter the dining area.

Guests arrive at our front door, where they are told about our one item, one price approach. The all-inclusive price is $15.00 per person. There are no options. Everyone gets the same thing. If you don't like mashed potatoes and demand french fries instead, I'm sorry maybe you should go someplace else.

What about a lower priced child's plate?

No.

One size fits all and everybody pays the same price.

That's the novel concept that makes everything run smoothly. There's no menu to study, payment can and will be made when entering rather than leaving.

The number in the party, their dining area and table number is transmitted to the kitchen and the servers immediately.

Each party's table is made ready complete with a pitcher of iced tea and another of iced water just moments before the host introduces them to their server who seats them and pours their beverage.

The salad service tray pops out of the 'dumb waiter' as they are seated. It consists of a properly chilled iceberg lettuce salad topped with two tomato wedges and shaved carrot curls slathered with French dressing, hot yeast dinner rolls, butter and a bowl of site-prepared strawberry or peach jam depending on the season.

The servers' primary job is to bring food to the table, replenish drinks and condiments and clear the table. They do not take orders, present checks or deal with the kitchen in anyway.

At the conclusion of the meal, the servers bid the guests goodbye, clear the table, spread a fresh table cloth, set and refresh the table.

Luncheon service will begin at 11:30AM and conclude at 2:00PM. We do aerial demonstrations at 12:30PM and again at 1:30PM. If all works well we'll get two turns.

I would like each dining area to accommodate 12 four top tables. In round numbers that gives me the capability of serving 400 guests on each of the five days a week we plan to be open."

"So a max of $1,500,000 per year at 100% of capacity. That's not likely to happen. What do you think is realistic?" Reba was more than curious.

"My business plan is built on a third of that. Half a million dollars a year in revenue will net $250,000 a year. The magic comes from controlling costs very closely. That is why this must be a totally green restaurant. Utility cost must be zero."

Madison grinned broadly as he spoke, "We're totally with you on that. The cistern I mentioned will provide 100% of the buildings

water. The soil percolation tests are typically very, very good in
the La Grange area. Hence we will be able to use a large septic
tank with an oversized drain field for sewage.

The roof-top deck you want will force us to place a solar panel
field at ground level on the other side of the parking lot. As you
know, the panel material is black and absorbs heat. That's a bad
thing as heat reduces the panel's efficiency. We have had some
recent success with pumping fresh water from a secondary cistern
system across the reverse side of the panels to capture some of that
heat and cool the panels. The water is then flowed through a series
of pipes buried ten feet below the parking lot. The temperature at
that depth is a constant 56 degrees which is cool enough to bring
the water back to a low enough temperature to be re-introduced
into the secondary cistern. During winter, the chilling loop is
bypassed and the warmed water is pumped through solar heaters
mounted alongside the photovoltaic panels. Once the temperature
is elevated to 120 degrees it is directed to the pipes that we will
install in the buildings flooring."

"That's more than I need to know young Madison. I am counting
on you guys to make this building totally green so I can advertise
that to the folks who care. That'll give them a reason to come and
see what we've done.

While we're on that line, I want us to include eight recharging
spots for electric cars. Can we reach out to Tesla and see if they
would like to put one of their recharging stations here as well? If
they say no can we engineer two of our electric spots to do high-
speed charging equal to what Tesla does at their sites?"

Jenny jumped in, "Milton can we get back to a couple of points
about the restaurant?"

"Sure what have you got?"

"Do you see the dining areas as a series of small intimate spaces or
big open halls?"

"Big and open."

"What about the floors, wood or carpet or stone or what?"

"Well I really want dark hardwood but I worry about the noise."

"Don't, we can handle that in other ways.

There will have to be an elevator for the handicapped. Do you want stairs as well or shall we expand the size of the elevators for everyone's use?"

"I love stairs and I hate the handicapped issue. Isn't there a way around all of that?"

"We'll work on it.

More importantly what about the windows? Glass panels all across the back or a re-creation of the multi-paned ones that are in it now?"

"Multi-paned. Always remember this is a trip to Grandma's house."

"OK, we've got enough to work with and now we need to get back to the drawing board."

"Later Steve, Madison, Jenny. You guys are the absolute best."

The walk to Milton's Cherokee took longer than the flight back to La Grange. Neither Reba nor Milton spoke. They were each lost in their thoughts. The details of the project were catching up with them.

Reba's phone rang.

"Hey Daddy. What's up?"

"Well you've got trouble. Turns out that La Grange's Public Works Director and all around screwball, Charles Reed Brown is in McFarland's pocket, he's not going to issue Milton's water and sewer permits without a fight and that's a fight we probably can't win.

Digging a water well isn't much of an option either given the depth of the water table. Milton would have a better shot at hitting oil."

"Thanks Daddy. Next time you see Charles Reed Brown just look plenty worried. Let him think he's got us."

"Reba, are you saying he doesn't?"

"We're good."

"Daddy, please keep working on the city and the airport board for funding."

"I've got some of that done already. Let Milton know he's got his billboards and a grant of $50,000 to advertise and I almost forgot $200,000 for construction if he agrees to hire a minimum of 10 employees. I'll have the funds deposited into his account at my bank tomorrow afternoon."

"Daddy you're the best!"

Opening Day

Eventually planning and praying must give way to doing. The chase of perfection is abandoned and the prize of good enough accepted. The **Chickenfried Café** would open on March 1st as planned.

Marketing was priority number one for Milton. Everything else was a distant number two. Many roads lead to business success all of them are dependent on customers showing up and leaving money. No one understood that better. First they had to come then they had to return over and over again.

"So Milton, what was your marketing plan and how did you implement it?" Angela's voice projected an almost adoring interest.

"First let me say that marketing is fundamental to the **Chickenfried Café**. Our approach is constantly evolving. I'll go back to the beginning and tell you what we did then.

In those days we believed that our target market existed in three pools: local residents, roadway transients and affinity groups which included but importantly was not limited to pilots. The **Chickenfried Café** was and is aviation themed not aviation focused.

Nothing that I envisioned was revolutionary or unknown. The big difference was simply that I acted on what everyone else in the airport restaurant business knew should be done. Doing not merely strategizing was and still is the Joker in our deck.

For example, the FAA makes it easy to address the pilot community by providing a name and address list of **ALL** licensed pilots and **ALL** airworthy aircraft for **FREE**. The same is true of airports. Each is useful. We developed aviation sector specific postcards, posters and brochures. Every pilot within three hundred miles of La Grange received a postcard from us twice in the month prior to our opening date and once monthly thereafter. Pilots who own aircraft and base their aircraft within 100 miles of La Grange are mailed every week.

The core message is simple:
1. The **Second Best Chickenfried Steak in Texas**.
2. **No tipping**
3. **FREE** airshow daily
4. Pilots eat for **FREE**
5. Open Tuesday thru Saturday 11:30AM – 2:00PM
6. www.chickenfriedcafe.com

Airports, FBOs and flight schools were mailed small wall posters and brochures. I personally telephoned the owner or manager of every airport located business on our list to tell them about our restaurant and to invite them to stop by.

Today our outreach to the pilot community continues. They are our unpaid entertainers. The paying customers come to see these guys up close and to watch the planes they fly in action.

Then and now, every pilot who flies in for the first time, leaves with a **FREE Chickenfried Café** t-shirt. A cap comes with the second visit. After five, they become a member of the **Chickenfried Café Pilot's Club** which gives them **Planeload Pricing**. Everyone in their plane eats for $30.

I take two photos with each pilot on their first visit. One by the statue of **Chickenfried Chuck** and the other by their plane, both are posted on our website and tacked to our wall of honor. Naturally we print and send a set of framed 5x7's to the pilot. Our aim is to make them part of our family."

"What's the **Chickenfried Chuck** statue?"

"**Chickenfried Chuck** is our mascot. The statue is a 10 foot tall fiberglass rendering of a cow with wings in a roster pose, wearing a leather flying cap, aviator goggles and a flowing white silk scarf. Chuck is the original Skygod. Jenny, our young architect intern, came up with the concept and got some A&M art students to put it together.

Pilots are an affinity group. So are Car and Motorcycle Clubs. La Grange is in the middle of the Houston, Austin, San Antonio golden triangle. 11,500,000 people can drive to it within ninety minutes.

When we learn about a Corvette or Harley Club in Houston we invite them to come and schedule a day for their special event. We put their name up in lights on our billboards, which alerts other clubs that we don't know about to the possibility of an interesting outing for their crowd. Consider the possibilities.

Our core business though comes from the locals. We plastered La Grange with posters. Every business on the square had one in its window, many still do. Even other restaurants put one up. The logic is pretty simple. Getting people excited about eating out is good for everyone's business. Nothing causes a stir like something new. The kicker was to convince them that we weren't competition as we only serve one meal a day and are closed Sunday and Monday. It worked because it's the truth.

I met with every community leader and spoke at a meeting of every civic club and church group. The message on our billboards changed weekly to make certain that every passerby knew our opening date and why they wanted to be there. **FREE** was the central word.

FREE Airshow.
FREE pilot training.
FREE t-shirts.
FREE dessert.
FREE iced tea.
FREE salad.

The day before our opening we hosted a chickenfried steak eating contest on the town square. The winner walked away with heartburn and $10,000. In the sky above, the Piper J3 Cub I purchased for the daily airshows did banner towing duty. The message was simple – **Chickenfried Café**.

We had PRed the event heavily throughout our golden triangle. More stations then I could have hoped for in Houston, Austin and San Antonio talked it up. A chickenfried steak eating contest in Texas is very cool and a very big deal! TV crews from as far away as Dallas showed up to grab tape for the evening news.

TV news directors are overworked and underappreciated. Knowing that provided a post opening day opportunity. I brought in a video crew with a high haired, short skirted freelance reporter from Austin to film the opening day crush, some interior shots, airport traffic and the airshow. They pieced it together into 30 and 60 second segments which we squirted to every station in Texas. A few ran with it. PR is a game of inches.

Highway 71 and 77 intersect about a mile from our airport which fronts on Highway 71. The J3 takes to the air every morning at 10AM. It cruises up and down both of those roads while towing our banner to whet motorists' appetite and remind them of our presence.

"What about social media?" Angela's youth couldn't let her resist asking.

"We check all the boxes: Facebook, Twitter, Pinterest, YouTube even Instagram. To that we add our website and weekly blog.

Does social media help us is a better question? On that one, the jury is still out.

There is one thing that we do that is amazingly productive, email addresses. We collect and categorize them. Email campaigns are conducted based on relevance.

Here's an example. A year after our opening the **Chickenfried Café Food Bus** came into being. One of its benefits is the ability to support flyout adventures to places pilots might enjoy. An example is the Mooney factory in Kerrville. We work on a plant tour date with them and the use of their ramp. Pilots come, we feed them and they have an experience that is not generally available. We've done similar events with car clubs, sailing clubs and even spelunkers. I have no idea why anyone would want to crawl around in a cave but that's their thing. Mine is to feed them and grab their attention.

Here's the kicker, every time we do anything that might be of the slightest interest to the media, print, electronic or new we send every reporter and editor on our list a press pack, which includes the story, quotes, pictures, sound and video. We get more than our share of ink."

"So tell me about opening day. How do you remember it?"

"Well, Tom Joiner is a rat but he was right about converting an old house into a restaurant being a basket of compromises and that the finished product would be very different from what I had imagined.

It was so much better than I had dared to dream.

Madison and Jenny earned every bit of the 'A' that Steve gave them."

"Reba and I were still working late into the night the day before our opening. Finally I cried uncle and said, 'Reba, mash that elevator button and take us to the rooftop.' I had a bottle of really good red wine and two glasses for a private celebration."

"Milton, I've gotta' go. I'm really, really tired and tomorrow is going to be an incredibly busy day. Rain check?"

"Rain check it is. You could just stay here you know."

"Is there a ring and a proposal wrapped up in that offer?"

She waited for a reply that didn't come.

"What time will you be here in the morning?"

"Well I don't know. I want to be here when Steve lands."

"Steve? Why's he coming?"

"Because I invited him, who knows he may bring a ring and a proposal."

"That hurt."

"Good. I'll see you at 9:00AM."

"I'll be here."

Madison and Jenny had built a small owner's apartment adjacent to the roof top dining area. I had moved in before construction was finished and quickly developed the habit of sitting on the deck every night and watching the stars. During my days in California I could count the stars I could see on the fingers of one hand. In La Grange, they were as numerous as the grains of sand on a beach.

It would have been a perfect way to end the day if Reba had remained. She didn't and probably never would. She needed a proposal and a ring. Milton smiled knowing that very soon she'd have both.

The cooks arrived at 7:30AM to begin the prep. Everything that is served is made from scratch including the yeast rolls and the pecan pie. Max LeGran and Michael Grayson would take care of the hot kitchen while Jose Montoya and Louisa Bias managed the cold kitchen.

Max peeled potatoes while Michael trimmed the beef they'd be using to the appropriate size and ran it through the tenderizer. It went into the machine as half inch thick round steak and came out much thinner and looking something like the tread from an off-road tire. The next step was simply to add salt, pepper and garlic powder to each side and let it stand for 30 minutes before sending it back to the refrigerator.

At 10:30AM Max fired-up the fryer. The idea is to have the oil at the proper temperature and standing by before it's needed. Chickenfried steak cooks in six minutes. In a good restaurant food is prepared to order not to inventory. That's the way we do it, a dining room server signals the kitchen when the salad is presented. At that moment, the tenderized round steak is pulled from the refrigerator, dusted with seasoned floor, bathed in egg wash, dusted once again and gently placed in the fryer. The oil bubbles immediately as the steak tumbles and rolls. Soon it rises to the surface and remains there signifying completion.

As it is removed, drained and plated the race begins to serve. If the order is for a party of four all four must be cooked and served together. Timing is everything. Each steak must be tender and juicy inside with a crispy, golden crust.

Mashed potatoes and gravy are a different matter. They needed to be made in advance and keep warm without drying out the potatoes or crusting the gravy, art not science.

Yeast rolls are tricky as they need time to rise but must be baked before rising too much. To make the game a little more challenging, rolls are best when served hot out of the oven, science not art.

Green beans are all about feel and look. Ours are steamed over a boiling pot of ham and onion broth. The flavor is amazing.

On opening day, the servers arrived on schedule at 10:30AM. Each was dressed as a Pan Am Airlines stewardess from many years before. They looked sharp. Their presence added to the something special nature of the dining experience Milton was creating. Lunch was about to takeoff. Happy landings!

All of the servers were young, fit, female college students with pleasing personalities. Their training went constantly to one point and only one point. **The customer is king.** He pays your salary treat him well. Respect is something you give, not something you expect. Check your attitude at the door. Be an actor if you have to but be pleasant and respectful no matter what.

The host and hostess prepared to greet every guest at the front door, accept their payment, find them an appropriate table and show them to it. Both were dressed in aviator outfits from a long ago time, he as a Pan Am Captain and she as the Chief Stewardess.

"Places everyone" Reba announced excitedly.

Weeks before Milton had planned for this moment. Opening Day, indeed opening week and opening month had to succeed and do so big time.

"You must have had some problems figuring out the product formula. Did everything really go perfectly on opening day?" Angela asked incredulously.

"I'm an optimist and tend not to dwell on life's speed bumps.

Telling every pilot within three hundred miles that there was such a thing as a **FREE** lunch, brought a much bigger crowd than we ever imagined. Buck's ramp and ours hit capacity before 10AM."

Buck burst into my kitchen like a wildman with his hair on fire, "Moooz you gotta' do something. The sky is filled with arriving airplanes, the ramp is full-up and the pilots are getting plenty pissed."

"Park 'em in the grass alongside the taxi way. We'll send one of our golf cars to ferry them to the FBO office. Will that work?"

"I don't know. Let's try it."

"Ask Reba to call Pastor Dave and see if he can truck over a load of folding tables and chairs from the church. If so, can we set them up in your big hangar? We've got way too many pilots to feed at our Skygods' Table."

"Yeah that'll work I'll get on it."

"Looks like we're going to get hammered by success, more people are coming than we could have imagined.

I've got plenty of food and plenty of help the problem is seats.

Kelly Evans, one of our beautiful and bright servers came up with the answer before anyone went hostile."

"Mr. Muzny if we serve dessert on paper plates. People can stroll the flight line, look at the airplanes watch the airshow and enjoy their slice of pecan pie al at the same time."

"Perfect solution, Kelly, people linger and visit over dessert. This will get them moving quickly without feeling rushed. You get today's lemonade out of lemons award."

Angela smiled and said "That was a creative solution. Did it work?"

"Like a charm. The pilots joined up by staying with their airplanes and telling the folks that wandered by about them. We couldn't have planned it better.

Opening day was a success as was opening week and opening month. Then we got hit with three mighty blows that almost sank us."

Jean-François

"Tell me about the culinary genius, Jean-François Fournier, who works for you?" Angela began to dig deeper into the business side of this overnight success story.

"No one knew much about Jean-François, where he came from, what he did or who he knew. He just drifted into town unannounced and showed up at the **Chickenfried Café** a week after we opened. Everyone accepted that he was French given his thick accent and acerbic personality. All of the boxes on the French stereotype list got checked in his case.

In those days, I was the chief cook. Everything had to be done according to a recipe I concocted and a procedure I developed. My house, my rules.

The kitchen door swung open on our second Tuesday with a wild eyed, screaming Frenchman moving through it …….."

"You cooked this?" snarled Jean-François Fournier.

"I surely did. Is there a problem?"

"It is flat. Did you season it or merely rely on what nature provided for free?"

"You're French aren't you?"

"Yes, does that matter?"

"It might explain your attitude. You're welcome to eat here but you need to tone down the rudeness."

"Rude? You think I am being rude because I tell you the truth about your food?"

"Look wise guy do you think you can do better?"

"No I don't think I can, I know I can. Let me prove it to you. Let me into your kitchen and I'll prepare your menu for the next five people that show-up. They'll be the judge. If they like what I've cooked and you agree then you have to hire me."

"So you're looking for a job?"

"I wasn't when I came in, now I am. You're running a restaurant the way I always wanted to; one dish you believe in, served at lunch, no dinner. It is the only way to bring great food to the masses – haute cuisine from an assembly line."

"OK Frenchy, on one condition."

"What's that?"

"You must pay for the meals of the customers you serve. If they hate the food I don't lose money."

"OK, let's get busy. May I see the kitchen?"

Soon a party of five arrived and was seated. They had been here three times in our first week and knew what to expect.

Salad, yeast rolls and iced tea came immediately.

Jean-François was busy in the kitchen. Milton wandered around the dining rooms and chatted up his guests with special interest in table 21 where the special five were seated. He knew them.

"Hope you guys came hungry."

"We did Milton and you never disappoint."

"You're very kind." Feeling odd about doing a *'guinea pig'* test with his guests, Milton's face uncontrollably grimaced.

Jean-François motioned for a server and presented the five plates and gravy boat he had prepared for table 21.

Carol Ann Womack, the chosen server, looked at the tray before her and wondered. Everything appeared the same but the aroma was more inviting, the crust coating the meat was more golden and the string beans glistened brightly. Something had changed.

Jean-François motioned for her to hurry. Food, good food **MUST** be served immediately.

As Carol Ann set a plate before each guest, an uncommanded smile lightened their faces as they glanced at her with questioning eyes. The slight changes were being noticed.

Big Ed was served first and chose not to wait for the others. He grabbed the gravy boat with the fervor of the last arrival at a boarding house table and spilled the creamy sauce on his steak and mashed potatoes being careful to avoid polluting his green beans. Hunting his first bite, the crust snapped as he sliced through. He watched the juices rush onto his plate from the tender steak inside. Anxiously he shoved the first bite into his quivering pie hole.

"The word's *'man that's good'* loudly escaped his mouth before he finished chewing. That was the signal for the other members of the family to begin.

Each agreed with Big Ed. Martha the pearl of his life for the last 25 years caught a glimpse of Milton out of the corner of her eye.

She called him over and offered, "This is the best meal we've ever had in La Grange. Now you'll have to change the big sign on the highway which promises *'the second best chickenfired steak in Texas!'* as this is surely the best our great state has to offer."

Milton smiled, "Thank you Martha, and what about you Big Ed was your meal OK?"

"Hell no! I feel cheated. I've come in here three times and been served second best each time. Why did you wait so long to upgrade me? Has everybody else been getting this all along and you singled me out for punishment? What did I ever do to piss you off?"

Big Ed Wallace wasn't a man to speak softly and carry a big stick. He shouted at you and hit you with the stick at the same moment leaving nothing to chance. Everyone in the restaurant heard his complaint and everyone wanted to know exactly what was up.

Johnson the Small rushed in from his table on the airplane watching deck. "What's up, Big Ed?"

"Milton's been cheating me, you too probably. Taste this!"

Lance Johnson did exactly as Big Ed commanded. He chewed for a moment on the fork full he was given from the little that was left on Big Ed's plate. Before he could speak and render an opinion Big Ed jammed a spoonful of mashed potatoes smothered with gravy into the middle of his mouth.

Johnson the Small uttered only one word, "Amazing."

Milton knew how to turn a lemon into lemonade, "Ed, it's my fault for sure and I was unfair with you. I'm testing a new recipe and I wanted your opinion of it. You're the first person in all of Texas to taste it. Sounds like I'm on the right track. How about I have Carol Ann bring your family seconds, on the house?"

"Did I hear *'Stingy'* Milton offer seconds? Bring 'em on Carol Ann before the tight wad changes his mind."

Milton raced back to the kitchen to find Jean-François.

"Chef you got yourself a job. Now cook up 75 more of those steaks, a pot of the mashed potatoes, mess of beans and a cauldron of gravy. I've got no idea what you did but the people sure like it."

"No!"

"No? What do you mean no? No, what?"

"No, I won't cook anything until you have agreed to my terms and I accept the position."

"So this is a shakedown? How much do you want?"

"It isn't about money. It has to do with breakfast."

"Breakfast?"

"Yes, breakfast."

"We don't serve breakfast."

"That's a problem for me. I can't work at a place that doesn't serve breakfast. I need to start my day preparing breakfast."

"Look Frenchy. I started this place to do things my way and my way doesn't include breakfast. I serve one meal a day – lunch and only one thing for lunch – chickenfried steak. I don't want to sell breakfast."

"First, never call me Frenchy again my name is Jean-François. You must show respect to me by calling me by my name and I must serve breakfast."

"Look I'm a reasonable man, I'll listen. What would breakfast look like?"

"Beignets, Chicory coffee, plain and chocolate milk and nothing else. I imagine the coffee to be served Black or Au Lait which is a mix of half coffee and half hot milk. The Beignets will be prepared and presented exactly as they are served at Café du Monde in New Orleans' French Market. Mine are better."

"Are we talking about that 150 year old café just off Jackson Square?"

"We are."

"I like that place. It is because of them that I have the green and white canvas awning over our airplane watching deck out back. I love the way it looks."

"I do too. It was your awning that made me envision serving beignets and chicory coffee here each morning. This setting is better than theirs. It is peaceful"

"How about orange juice?"

"No it isn't reasonable to expect to get good quality oranges every day. We could not meet the high standards that our guests will expect from us."

"OK, Fren… I mean Jean-François. Let's shake on it. Now can you please cook up seventy-five chickenfried steak dinners?"

They shook hands. The deal was done. The **Chickenfried Café's** success was assured. At least Milton and Jean-François thought so.

Jean-François commanded the line cooks, the scullery workers, the bus boys and the servers as a general drilled a great army. He quickly molded this group of head strong individuals into a one for all and all for one team. His mission was to bring forth the best restaurant in Texas from this simple diner. Today marked the beginning of a journey not the arrival at success.

Soon everyone who had come for lunch had a second helping which most insisted on paying for as it was the best meal they had ever had and they didn't want the place to fold for lack of cash.

Two o'clock came, the door closed, the sign was flipped from *'Open'* to *'Closed'*. Inside there was jubilation. Everyone knew that a corner had been turned today and that from now on things would only get better and better and busier and busier.

All businesses are built on the foundation of a great product. They now served *'**The Best Chickenfried Steak in Texas**'.* Even so, Milton would never change the sign on the highway or the slogan on the menu. Giving people more than they were conditioned to expect was the path he had always walked and that would never change.

Soon the restaurant cleared out except for Jean-François and Milton. The boss wouldn't make the daily three o'clock flight to his secret FiveOnFive Ranch today. He wanted to come to better know the Frenchman who had made such a tremendous contribution to the success of the **Chickenfried Café** and done so in just one lunch.

"Jean-François where did you learn how to cook?"

"I never formally studied culinary arts if that is what you are asking. All Frenchmen learn cooking from their families. My grandfather was my principle guide when it came to technique. I learned by watching him slice, chop, mix, stir, sauté, fry and bake. He was a master. My grandmother did the shopping. Together we would go to the market in our village or one nearby. She would examine what was fresh each day. Eggs, cucumbers, lamb and fish were all studied with equal care. Appearance, touch and smell each told their part of a story leading to a purchase or exclusion. Good was never good enough for her only the best would do.

I learned to show my love for my family and friends by the care I took to prepare a meal or a simple loaf of bread."

"So you grew up with food?"

"As do we all, the difference for me was learning that great food should be part of everyday life not something to be saved for special occasions."

"So if not food what did you study?"

"I did study food but not how to cook it. I am a biophysicist."

"What in the world is that?"

"Biophysicists study the chemical and physical properties of living things and the biological processes that affect them.

My work and interests focus on the effects of substances such as drugs, hormones, and food on tissues and biological processes."

"Still?"

"Still and always, it is my passion. Because of it, I am able to create amazing dishes that people want to eat."

"I don't understand."

"Look at it this way. God designed us to be drawn to pleasure and withdraw from pain and unpleasantries. Our sensory organs inform us which is which.

When we eat, all five senses are involved; sight, sound, touch, smell and taste. It is one of a few human activities where that is true. Music for instance is strictly about sound.

For the moment, let's focus only on taste and smell. To make food taste better it is necessary to know exactly how the body works. A biophysicist knows that and a chef doesn't, so each approaches the presentation of great food differently."

"So how does the body taste?"

"Simply put, our mouth is loaded with microscopic receptor/transmitter cells that we commonly call taste buds.

Am I moving too fast?"

"No I'm with you so far."

"Good. In simple terms our taste receptors are specialized. Some sense sweet but only sweet, others sense savory but only savory, add to that temperature sensors so we know about hot and cold."

"I understand but how does that apply to selling food?"

"Let me tell you a story that you'll find both interesting and informative.

In his book, **Grinding it Out**, Ray Kroc tells us the story of how he bought a single hamburger diner in Riverside, California and turned it into the corporate powerhouse we know as McDonalds. Clearly the best and most loved product they ever produced is the simple french-fry. No restaurant before or since makes one that equals McDonalds.

Here's why?

In the early days, there was a potato bin behind the Riverside location. A mountain of potatoes was kept there. Twenty four hours before they were to be fried and sold, each was peeled, sliced and soaked in a bucket of water. The press that did the slicing was designed to produce perfectly sized french fires. Each about the size of a number two pencil, though square not round. The water they were soaked in was saturated with sugar, ordinary table sugar.

After twenty four hours of soaking they could be fried and served according to the McDonald brothers' cook to inventory formula. They had to be hot and ready when the customer ordered them and thrown away if they remained in inventory for longer than twenty minutes."

"So where's the biophysics in that?" Milton asked.

"Remember we are primarily discussing the sense of taste. Most french-fries served in this world are merely fried potatoes, which are very bland. It is the nature of potatoes. To liven them up a bit they are liberally salted.

Our savory taste buds are fired when they are touched by the salt. It follows our design path. A pleasure sensor is fired and we are pleased. It is this way for most french-fries of the world. A bland uninteresting food becomes desirable because of salt.

Now McDonald's comes along and adds sugar which has been soaked into its french-fries for twenty-four hours prior to cooking. Salt is added after cooking.

What happens to taste?

Twice as many receptors are fired, those that sense savory salt and those that sense sweet sugar. Simply put twice as many receptors firing equals twice the sensation of pleasure to our brains. We don't taste the sugar as it is overpowered by the salt. This is why we so prefer the McDonalds french-fry to every other french-fry.

Add to this the fact that sugar when subjected to heat becomes golden brown hence the remarkable color of the McDonald's french-fry and its crispness. So the senses of sight, taste and touch all conspire to heighten our pleasure when eating a simple bag of fries.

Another company, Starbucks, unlocked the same secret and learned to use it to their economic benefit. They involve even more mouth based sensory receptors and are further benefitted by the sense of smell. Coffee is savory; sugary products like caramel and whipped cream are added. That combo fires as many receptors as a McDonalds french-fry. Additionally they benefit from the heat receptors excited by the hot coffee and the cold receptors set off by the cool whipped cream. Caffeine, a mildly addictive narcotic, completes Starbucks winning formula. It works!

If either company had consulted a biophysicist they would have arrived at the same or similar formula. Neither did as far as I know. They made fortunate, accidental discoveries and dominate their market segments as a result."

"Let me guess. You used your knowledge of biophysics to enhance my recipes and generate the rave responses we got at lunch today. Correct?"

"Partially correct, I am also a good cook armed with the techniques to properly incorporate the biophysical magic. I don't like to think of the kitchen as a laboratory or the customers as a control group but on this day it was exactly what each became."

"What specifically did you do?"

"First I read and understood your recipes. They are good ones.

To your chickenfried steak batter I added sugar, a bit more salt and removed the pepper entirely. Knowing that the sugar enriched batter would brown more quickly caused me to respond by reducing the cooking time. I increased the tenderization of the meat to allow it to cook more quickly while preserving its juices. No one admires a dry, tough piece of meat.

Viola, it worked!

The crust was the golden brown of a McDonalds french-fry and the meat was juicy.

I am unhappy with the thinness of the steak that I had to use and look forward to buying better marbled beef which will permit a thicker portion without increasing cooking time."

"What did you do to achieve the smoothness of the mashed potatoes?"

"It is an old French trick. Sour cream is used rather than butter. Heat causes butter to reduce rapidly to a watery consistency. Sour cream maintains its texture and transfers it to the potatoes. I want a smooth rich texture that will maintain its shape on the plate. Care must be taken to not over mix, which captures and folds in air for the moment and then deflates before our customers' disbelieving eyes and spurs the displeasure of their tongue. Only proper cooking techniques can produce the mouth feel that biophysics demands.

I will not bore you further by explaining the treatment of the green beans or the gravy. They too are given respect by combining the science of biophysics with the art of cooking."

"Well done sir well done.

How shall I pay you?"

"Frequently and generously I trust."

"You'll earn either ten percent of the net or five percent of the gross. You decide which. I'll guarantee $4,000 a month no matter which you choose."

"It is easier to calculate against gross then net. So let's live with that. I assume that you will want me involved in the other restaurants as well and will pay me the same amount for each of them."

"There are no other restaurants."

"Soon there will be."

"Jean-François, when do we start serving breakfast?"

"Next Friday."

"Next Friday it is."

Milton said good night for they had talked well beyond evening. He pulled out his phone and punched Reba's icon.

"Hey Milton, I heard about your day twenty times already. My phone keeps ringing with the news of your latest success.

Way to go."

"Can I round up enough money to open another location?"

"I'd say so. When and where?"

"Someplace near Dallas but I'm not exactly sure which place yet. Go ahead and round up some cash. We'll head up that way next Wednesday."

"How are you gonna' get the time off?"

"Jean-François Fournier."

"Sounds like you went out and got yourself a number two."

"Actually he came looking for me."

"Life's like that."

Horsemeat

"Did you open **Chickenfried Café #2** in the Dallas area?" Angela asked in her best investigative reporter's voice.

"No. Number three went into the Dallas Area as did numbers 4 and 5. Muskogee, Oklahoma became home to **Chickenfried Café #2**."

"Why?"

"Two reasons. First, like La Grange it sits in the middle of a golden triangle, smaller to be sure but golden none the less. Over four million people call the Oklahoma City, Tulsa, Ft. Smith triangle home. Many of them fly and most love airplanes. Additionally, it is an easy flight from Dallas which would allow us to begin building buzz in the metroplex and help us pick the right launch point in that key market.

It took us six months to find, design, build and open #2. That was disappointing but it taught us how to open #3 and #4 in just 60 days."

"Why did #2 take so long?"

"We couldn't count on finding, moving and renovating old buildings forever and if we tried, each location was likely to be different in appearance and functional form which would be a training, operational and branding nightmare. The design team came up with a new build alternative that made sense but it took a while to land on it. The design needed to be scalable and economical while never sacrificing the Grandma's house look, inside or out. We're now able to open a restaurant thirty days after striking a deal with an airport."

"How did you free up the time to open new locations so quickly after launching?"

"The short answer is Jean-François.

He quickly became indispensable. Not only did he know about food and how to prepare it but he also was an expert at restaurant operations. First he took over the staff; hired, fired, trained and scheduled. Then he created special events as a marketing outreach to the community. Women flocked to him likes bees to honey. I think it's his French accent. At any rate, Jean-François came to me one afternoon and said he wanted to do a wine tasting, featuring local wines. The hill country is saturated with boutique vineyards.

Soon it was part of our monthly schedule. People drove down from Austin and flew in from as far away as New Orleans. It just worked and we sold a ton of wine.

Next he started cooking seminars featuring breads, pastries and soufflé's. Somehow he made it all look easy and everyone who came left feeling accomplished. Soon a small portion of our first floor dining room was set aside as a product sales area; wines, hard to find cooking utensils, cook books, pecan pies and eventually cheese.

It was the cheese that almost put us out of business. Jean-François's brother lives in the small village of Céreste, located in the sunny Provence region of southern France. Convinced that good cheese only comes from France, Jean-François arranged for his brother to ship over several pounds of the best his area had to offer. He began offering cheese and wine tastings every other Friday. To his credit they were a hit. Soon cheese was added to the items available for sale in our ever expanding store."

"Milton, could we switch direction and discuss golf for a moment? Particularly FiveOnFive."

"Sure. FiveOnFive has been part of my life for many years though I didn't take the time to concentrate on it until I came to La Grange."

"I have only the spottiest information about your background in golf. Can you fill me in?"

"Sure no one in my family had ever picked up a golf club until I did at age twelve. I was instantly and forever hooked. Eventually I was given a scholarship to play golf at the University of Houston. It was a pretty darn good golf school in those days. To have some spending money I also taught golf lessons and have continued to do so until this day.

My teaching interest was to help folks who are really poor players to enjoy the game by first becoming 'ON PURPOSE GOLFERS' and 'BIG HOLE putters'.

'On purpose golfing' is a little bit like instrument flying. The whole idea is to make the golf ball or the airplane go exactly where you intend for it to go. For example, if you want an airplane to cruise at 5,000' you keep it at exactly five thousand feet and don't allow it to wander lazily between 4,500' and 5,500'. If you want to follow a course of 330 degrees then you hold the airplane exactly on that course, no excuses.

Golf is the same way. When you stand on the tee you pick a target, the exact spot where you want the ball to land. You then select a club from your bag that has the capability to get it there given your known ability. Bubba Watson can swing my clubs and make the ball go a lot further than I can. What matters is not how far he can hit it but how far I can. So I swing. If the ball lands exactly where I planned, I have won on that shot. If it goes anyplace else I have lost at 'on purpose golf'.

It makes me sick when I watch the pros play what passes for golf. They hit hard and their balls go long, very long but too often they land in a sand trap, sometimes in the rough, sometimes in the trees and only occasionally in the middle of the fairway. They're professionals and they should be able to make their ball go where they want it to go every time. They don't. The first thing I do with a new student is make them promise to stop watching golf tournaments on television.

Most of what I teach has to do with 'Big Hole Putting'.

Do you play?"

"I do."

"That's a good thing. As you know, golf courses are designed so that half of all the strokes a player should take during a round are taken on the green. If we're on the standard par 72 golf course then we know that 36 of all the strokes we take today should occur on the green. That's two putts per green. Two!

Getting a ball to enter a 4 inch cup from a hundred feet away can be tough. As a matter of fact it is almost impossible. But how about this, if the cup was ten feet in diameter anyone could putt it in from anywhere on the green without even considering how the green might break, couldn't they?"

"Yes Milton, I'd have to agree with that."

"Well that's the first thing I teach on the putting green. Imagine that the hole is in fact ten feet in diameter. I actually paint a ten foot circle on my teaching green so my students don't have to imagine, they can visualize.

Here's what happens next. The ball is putted and stops rolling somewhere inside that ten foot circle. Now let's consider what that means. Worst case the ball is five feet from the 4 inch cup, on average it is merely two and a half feet away. Two and a half feet!

We spend hour after hour practicing one, three and five foot putts. That's 'BIG Hole Putting' in a nutshell.

I can teach folks how to putt and win at it. I can teach them how to aim and put the ball at the spot they choose. What I have trouble teaching and have always had trouble teaching is the 'golf swing'. The reason is simple. There is no such thing and fundamentally can't be.

Here's why.

We are allowed 14 clubs in our golf bag. It breaks down this way:
1. Putter
2. 2-9 iron

3. Sand Wedge
4. Pitching Wedge
5. Driver
6. Three wood
7. Hybrid Wood

That's the lot, fourteen clubs. Here's the problem, each is of a different length, weight and loft. You can't address the ball in the same way with the long driver as you can with the short wedge. The lengths of those two club shafts are greatly different. So the swing which is defined by club length is different for each club in your bag. They all have a unique length. It gets worse. You have to be able to use a full swing, half swing and quarter swing with each. That adds up to a minimum of forty-two different swings.

Learning 'A' golf swing is possible but forty-two? That's a pipe dream for a weekend golfer.

One day long ago the simple fix hit me. Make all golf clubs in your bag the same length. Simple! The question was what length? The obvious answers are always the hardest to discover.

I had that answer when I arrived in La Grange. Two reasons caused me to stay. Reba was one. The other was the small ranch I owned in nearby Giddings, Texas. It was the perfect place to finish the development of my golf clubs in secret."

"Giddings though close is a long way from La Grange. How often were you able to get there to do the work?"

"Everyday.

The beauty of Giddings was the turf runway and hangar that existed there. About a month after I showed up in La Grange I purchased a J3 Cub for the airshow. Each day at 3:00PM I would fire it up and fly to Giddings without telling anybody where I was going. The plane would go into the hangar where I had a complete workshop which is not unusual for a small ranch. In it I cut the shaft of my driver to the length of my five iron. That was step number one. The length had been chosen and the first club modified.

The turf strip did double duty as a driving range. Quickly I learned that my redesigned golf clubs would require more work than simply making all the shafts the same length. I remember vividly addressing the ball for the first time with a shortened driver in what would normally have been the five iron position. The ball was teed-up exactly half way between my feet and about 18 inches away from my body. I used my five iron swing and the ball went straight but not very far and much higher than desired. The 'feel' was just south of awful. Tweaking was required, lots of tweaking.

For now I would have to divide my time between golf clubs in Giddings and the **Chickenfried Café** in La Grange. Goals, time dimensioned, quantified goals have to be set or nothing ever gets finished, at least not for me. So I set a goal to showcase my clubs at US Open Championship the following year.

About an hour before sundown each day, I would pull the J3 out of the hangar and onto the turf strip and fly back to La Grange in time for dinner with Reba."

"What was primary, the restaurant or the golf clubs?" Angela asked quizzically.

"The golf clubs by a narrow margin though both were edged out by the *Texas Zephyr*."

"What in the world is that?"

"We haven't come to it yet but we will. For now let me simply say that it is a hybrid airplane. Sort of like the Prius of the skies but unlike the Prius it is skewed more towards electricity and less towards gasoline.

I live life in full motion. It is normal for me to have several projects in motion at the same time, most of them fail. Starting things is what I'm good at, operating them not so much, hence my reliance on Jean-François and Reba. Every now and then things had a way of dragging me back into running the restaurant. At those moments I arrived kicking and screaming.

As I remember it happened that way one Thursday evening. I was on approach for La Grange in the J3 when I noticed a crowd of people and two police cars.

There are easier planes to taxi than a J3 Cub, practically all of them really. The reason is that the pilot of a J3 must sit in the rear seat when he's flying alone to keep the machine within its weight and balance envelope. That's not a problem in the air. You can see forward just fine. On the ground things are very different. The tail goes down and the nose goes up. The pilot's forward view is totally blocked. You must taxi the J3 slowly like all other taildraggers or you risk 'ground looping' it. The only way to see where you're going is to constantly do slight 'S' turns.

I saw Sheriff Larry Dinkins walking towards me as I entered the ramp and worried that I might run into him if he kept coming so I shut it down well short of the tiedowns. As I crawled out, which is the only way to get out of a J3, I felt his hand on my shoulder."

"Milton you've got a big problem with the Department of Health. There's a car load of state inspectors heading this way from Austin right now."

"I'm lost can you fill me in?"

"Did you really think you could get away with letting that crazy Frenchman serve horsemeat to your customers?"

"Horsemeat? What exactly are you talking about and where is Jean-François?"

"He's in the back of my patrol car right now."

"Is he under arrest for something?"

"No it's for his safety. Some of the people in the crowd are really upset."

"Come on Larry, take me through this slowly. What happened?"

"Sue Ellen Murphy brought her high school French class to lunch at your restaurant today. The upstairs dining room was reserved exclusively for them. After lunch, Jean-François met with them and did a presentation of French cheeses.

As they were leaving, Buck invited them to the flight line to meet Arnold Bowles who had just finished his final airshow performance of the day.

One of the students happened to see a discarded cardboard box labeled, 'viande de cheval' in your dumpster at the edge of the ramp. I am told 'viande de cheval' is French for 'horse meat'. I don't speak French but all of those kids do.

It gets better. They Tweeted photographs of that box and two others just like it.

I was contacted. The boxes are now in my possession and will be held in our evidence locker. The District Attorney is on his way out here to consider what charges to bring against you and Jean-François. For the time being I have padlocked your restaurant and you are officially out of business until further notice."

"Larry did you find any actual horsemeat in our refrigerators?"

"Maybe.

I've confiscated every scrap of meat in your place. It will be sent away for forensic testing to determine its origin; cow, pig or dog. If a man will cook a horse he'll probably cook a dog.

Milton you're truly disgusting. Most of us around here love horses. The idea of eating one makes us sick to our stomachs. The thought that we might have been fed someone else's horse without our knowledge makes us angry, really angry, Milton."

"Can I talk to Jean-François?"

"Heck no. The DA wants to interview him first."

Just then Reba pulled up, parked, walked past the crowd, gave Milton a hug and stood by his side.

"Hey Reba."

"Hey Milton. What's going on?"

"Oh just another day in paradise."

"So you don't need to talk to Daddy's criminal attorney friend, Guy Smyrle, because he's on his way over right now."

"Well it wouldn't hurt to talk, I suppose."

Guy was a man lost in time. His love of the past was made clear when he arrived driving a white 1970 MGB-GT. It was a semi cold day and he was wearing a Burberry trench coat and hat. He looked a lot like Peter Sellers stepping out of a Pink Panther movie. Everybody used to wear Burberry trench coats. No one does today, no one excepting Guy Smyrle. His ensemble was topped off with a seat of Polaroid aviator style dark glasses. Thirty or forty years ago Guy would have been a very cool guy but time has moved on. Today he just looks odd.

"Milton Muzny, this is Guy Smyrle.

Guy, shake hands with Milton Muzny." Reba did the introductions.

"Milton, is there someplace we can talk? Sure my hangar or Buck's conference room. Apparently my restaurant and my apartment are no longer available to me."

"Conference room works for me.

Sheriff Dinkins, I'm also representing that French boy. Are you going to let me talk to him now or later?"

"He's on ice until DA Earle talks with him."

Milton, Reba and Guy moved off in the direction of Buck's office.

Guy began, "Milton, Reba's Daddy has retained me to defend you. Do you accept me as your attorney in this matter?"

"I do."

"There's not much I can do until Ronnie Earle gets here and concludes his preliminary investigation. I'll push to get you back into your building and your apartment this evening. I don't think this is as big a deal as it looks right now. At least not criminally, your business will probably suffer."

Just then DA Earle knocked on the door with Jean-François in tow. "Guy, I've interviewed Jean-François and looked at the boxes, I just don't see that we've got a problem here.

Jean-François, just tell everyone what you told me."

"In my opinion, the best cheese in France comes from my small village and the surrounding countryside. My brother was kind enough to travel to many small farms in the area and buy cheeses for me. That was good. As they fell into three basic types, he packed them in three separate boxes which he then placed into a shipping crate.

My brother's neighbor is the town butcher. He supplied the boxes.

There was no horsemeat shipped from France to here just cheese in horsemeat boxes. The crate was opened, inspected and cleared customs as cheese not horsemeat. I provided Mr. Earle with the customs documents."

Guy jumped in, "So Ronnie what do you think? Do we need to stretch this thing out further or just shut it down?"

"Guy it's kinda' like a snowball rolling downhill. It gathers speed and size. If it were only me I'd say we're good but it isn't. The Health Department inspectors are coming down from Austin. Their investigation and action is a separate thing. I'm comfortable with what I've seen and heard but I can't speak for those guys."

"Ronnie can't you give them a call and fill them in. Maybe they'll just whip a U and head home."

"Could be, can somebody get me a number?"

"Let's you and me go ask Larry. I'll bet he's got it."

They left with Jean-François in trail.

Milton breathed deeply, laughed and asked Reba, "Now what?"

"Well you wanted marketing all to yourself and this feels like a marketing issue to me."

"I know. I'm thinking that we need to move quickly on restaurant #2. Social media has changed everything when it comes to crisis management. If the issue was confined to the kids in that classroom and the people they tell about what they saw. I could fix that easily and quickly. The problem is the Twitterverse. The Horsemeat Tweet is trending. I'm going to have to fight fire with fire and I'm not sure yet how to do that."

"You will. Let's sleep on it. Tomorrow we'll know."

"For now let's walk over and catch up with Guy, Ronnie and Larry.

They walked slowly but heard the laughter long before they reached the group.

"What's so funny guys?"

Sheriff Dinkina gave him the news, "We got hold of those boys from the State Department of Health to try to get them to call off the dogs. They said they wouldn't turn around because they have heard about the **Chickenfried Café** and are itching to have a meal here. I told them that you only did lunch not dinner. They said they were coming for dinner and if they didn't get dinner tonight nobody would get lunch tomorrow. I took the lock off the door and returned your meat to the refrigerator. Looks like you need to get busy."

"Thanks men. We're on it."

Reba, Milton and Jean-François put on aprons fired up the fryer and began the prep.

"Jean-François are you OK?" Milton had to know how quickly his star could rebound.

"Yes, yes I am fine. The whole affair seems silly to me. A horse is merely a cow without the horns. You American's are odd. How do you justify eating cows and protecting horses. They are cousins!"

"You just gave me the answer to our Twitter issue, Jean-François."

"What will you do?"

"We will embrace the horsemeat."

"What the heck does that mean?"

"First it is only the social media crowd that we have to worry about. Fixing the story with the locals and the pilot community will be easy. Except for the 'haters' and as the Taylor Swift song goes 'haters are gonna' hate' and there are some folks that just don't wish us well. They'll stir things up for a while and then it will die down. In the meantime, remember that any publicity is good publicity as long as they spell our name correctly. The Twitterverse is a horse of a different color; pun intended."

Reba still wasn't laughing, "Milton have you got any idea where #2 is going to be and when we'll get it started?"

"Muskogee, Oklahoma is my pick. I'm flying up there tonight to meet with the city council and the airport board tomorrow morning to see what we can work out. Reba I am hoping to use the same design team. Could you check in with Steve and see if there's any chance?"

"I'll make that proposal to Steve. I wonder what he'll propose to me and if it comes with a ring."

"Reba, have you got an itch to get hitched?"

"I do and you need to scratch it before somebody else does."

"So it's a horse race is it?"

"The only thing on your mind right now is horses, darn you. Jump into that 'ole Cherokee of yours and hit the trail. We'll talk when you get back."

"Ok Baby Girl, but first I've gotta' Tweet."

@ChichenfriedCafe Besieged by Frenchmen looking for horsemeat. ALL a hoax. We don't have any. Never did. #horsemeat #horsemeathoax #hoax

Problem solved.

Recipe

"By the end of the first year, the **Chickenfried Café** was a success but a smaller success than I could tolerate. I wanted it to be bigger, much bigger.

There were six restaurants, each with a small, on premise store selling branded **Chickenfried Café** merchandise. The **Chickenfried Chicken Coop**, our online store was up and running and beginning to contribute.

A success recipe had been discovered and duplicated." Milton beamed as he spoke. Pride wasn't central to his being but he was the proud papa of this baby.

"So what is the recipe?" Angela asked and had her next question at the ready as she was certain this one wouldn't be answered.

"First you must have a vision. Then you build a team. Finally, you create a product. A casual overview would lead you to believe that it's all about the product but it isn't. It's all about the team, for without the team there would be no product.

People come to us to be entertained and fed. They arrive looking for a good value. Our business is built on exceeding their expectations. That's what we do. Good enough has never been good enough.

My vision was to create an aviation themed restaurant at an aviation venue wrapped-up in a comfortable Grandma's house setting. Put in the vernacular of the Lone Star state, 'we danced with who brung us'. That has never changed. A couple of other things have."

"Really? What changed?"

"We moved from the lunch only concept to include Jean-François's Beignet breakfast system wide. Eventually, our lunch menu expanded to include **Chickenfried Chicken**. It's been a big hit. The rocking chairs that line the porch are now stained in a natural wood finish. They used to be painted white. Sure that's a small touch but details matter.

More important though is what has not been changed:

1. Our slogan – **The 2ⁿᵈ Best Chickenfried Steak in Texas**
2. Open Tuesday thru Saturday 11:30AM thru 2:00PM
3. **NO** tipping
4. **FREE** Airshow Daily
5. **FREE** Salad
6. **FREE** Iced Tea
7. **FREE** Pecan Pie
8. **FREE** Pilot Training
9. **FREE** food for transient pilots
10. Still just $15.00
11. Planeload pricing just $30.00

The biggest non-change is the food. It is the same today as it was when Jean-François arrived. Every meal we serve no matter where follows that formula. It works for us.

The airshow at every restaurant is performed by a classic bright yellow Piper J3 Cub. The routine is exactly the same, a few loops, some rolls, a 'balloon drop and prop pop' and a toilet paper shredding all done very low and very slow. An up close and personal visit with the leather flying capped, white silk scarf wearing pilot completes the show.

In an odd way it goes back to peoples need for bread and circuses the Emperors of ancient Rome discovered. Each brings happiness when served together euphoria."

"Can I quote you on that?"

"You better!

Our employees are the key ingredient to the **Chickenfried Café's** success recipe. We find them one at a time. Recruiting is made easier because we know what we're looking for in each position.

Every employee is a local. All of the servers are young, trim, attractive females. Jean-François hires and trains the kitchen staff and oversees our local vendor selections. We buy only local beef as the steaks we sell have never been frozen. Naturally pecans and potatoes are shipped in from a national supply source. They don't grow pecans in Michigan. If they did we'd buy them for our nearby restaurants. Reba hires and trains the host, hostess, manager and bookkeeper for each restaurant plus the three zone managers."

"You mentioned finding your people one at a time. Is there a common thread?"

"There is. Our folks care about other people. It is central to their character."

"How do you spot that?"

"We test for it by teaching our managers how to conduct a pre-employment interview. Ours is more of a screening out rather than a screening in process. It's like weeding a garden. The questioning begins by asking, 'how do you spend your time when you're not at work?' That's a pretty easy question but its answer speaks volumes. People who care about people spend time doing things with other people.

Next we focus on the job they're interviewing for by asking why they want the job. We never hire anyone whose entire answer centers on their need or desire for money. Everyone needs money but if that's the only reason for wanting a particular job you can't work for us. There has to be something about the job that is satisfying enough to provide the psychic income we all need from our vocations.

One of our dishwashers told me that he liked the immediate feedback of his job. He is given a tray of dirty dishes and he hands back a tray of sparkling clean ones. He takes pride in what he does. He needs the money but he loves his work. That's a true story, a dish washer that loves his work. Who'd have *thunk* it?

The design team eventually came up with a modular construction solution similar to the one used at the Hilton Palacio Del Rio on San Antonio's Riverwalk. In that case, every hotel room was made from pre-stressed concrete at a factory, trucked to the site and hosted into place. Our buildings are made of 14' by 40', steel and wood modules constructed in La Grange, trucked to their site and fastened together. Two modules make each floor. This process cuts construction costs and time by 50% while yielding a consistently perfect product.

The design is green. Each of our cafés provide 100% of their utility needs; power, water and sewage. Photovoltaic systems with battery and generator back-up provide the electricity. Water comes from cisterns supplemented by onsite wells. Sewage is moved to a large septic tank connected to an oversized drain field.

Each night the cooking oil we use in the fryers is recycled by passing it through a series particle sifts of decreasing size and then flowed through carbon filters. The result is *'can't tell it from new'* cooking oil which has no residual smell or taste from the previous days' use. The breakfast Beignets never taste like chickenfried donuts.

Believing that the best fertilizer for any crop is the footsteps of the owner and knowing that I can't possibly be at all places at the same time, we've gone super high tech. Every area of every restaurant is wired with cameras, speakers and microphones. I can literally monitor every operation in every restaurant in our system and make instant contact with our staff and guests if necessary. Jean-François can do the same thing. He has a personal presence in every kitchen.

Sales numbers flood into Reba's computer instantly from each restaurant. Inventory is controlled the same way. The moment a box of steaks is removed from a refrigerator, inventory is reduced.

All of the virtual stuff is great but I still have to make frequent personal appearances to keep things humming. Fortunately, all of our businesses are located at airports with instrument approaches.

My first thought was that I needed a faster more capable aircraft than my beloved Cherokee 300.

Figuring out what to replace it with was not easy. Today our restaurants in Southern California are over 1,000 miles away from our headquarters which is still in La Grange, Texas. That suggests a jet. The problem is I needed to buy more than one cross country capable airplane because I wasn't the only guy who needed to travel. It would be impractical to coordinate our travel plans closely enough to allow one jet to do the job for everyone.

Our insurance company had a cow when we mentioned that we might all travel on the same plane at the same time. No way. They would cancel our key man insurance. Reba's Daddy who is still our banker promised to cancel our loans if we all flew in the same plane at the same time. Some risks are too great to pass an actuarial peril assessment.

All of our restaurants are within 300 miles of at least one of our other locations. By managing travel as a scheduled event we could greatly reduce the performance expectations of the aircraft we might purchase.

My view was that no leg of any trip should exceed 3 hours. Speed and distance were far from the only issues in the travel equation. We wanted to be 'all weather' capable. I needed to know that our machines could get us where we needed to go and get us back to our starting place on schedule. As I saw it, we required planes that could go above 18,000' as that is the threshold of 80% of the world's weather. All turbo props and jets can do that but only piston powered aircraft that are turbo-charged can fill the bill as there isn't enough oxygen available above 18,000' to support combustion in a normally aspirated engine. For flights above 12,000' the FAA requires that non-pressurized aircraft be equipped with oxygen for the pilot and for the pilot and all passengers above 14,000'.

To function, the **Chickenfried Café** needed airplanes for each of our three zone managers."

"Why don't you just fly commercial? That's what I do!" Angela argued.

"Great question. None of our restaurants are at airports that accept commercial flights. If we flew commercial we would have to leave La Grange and go to a commercial airport to catch a flight to the commercial airport nearest the restaurant we planned to visit then rent a car and drive to the restaurant and repeat the process for our next meeting. Our travel would be less convenient and totally controlled by the airlines schedules not our own. It is hard to imagine being able to make more than one visit per day using commercial travel. If our restaurant visits average only one hour and they do then it is feasible for each of us to make up to three visits per day. Commercial air travel for us and for everyone else, I believe, is inefficient.

Uncle Sam was willing to pick up half the total purchase price of our new aircraft in the first year with a benevolent gift called Bonus Depreciation. I decided to accept his offer and planned to purchase new rather than used.

The decision making process was made easier but there were sparse product offerings in our wheelhouse. The Piper Matrix, Piper Meridian, Cirrus SR22T, Beechcraft 36GT, Cessna Corvalis TTx, Cessna 206T and the Cessna 182T were the contenders. After much study I decided to order three brand new Cirrus SR22T's with the GTS package.

I am often asked why? The answer is CAPS which stands for **Cirrus Airframe Protection System**. It's a full airframe parachute system. If things get seriously bad, it provides the way out. You pull the emergency handle, a rocket deploys a HUGE parachute and you descend safely to earth. I like that.

The cockpit has the comfort of a luxury vehicle. Each of our planes is equipped with air conditioning."

"I kept the Cherokee 300 for me, upgraded it a bit and still use it for most of my travel. A NetJets corporate travel program was added for our long range needs. They send a jet when we need it to take any of us where we need to go."

"Has everything worked out as you planned?"

"So far.

Our customer engagement philosophy is the main driver. We spend a lot of money on customer acquisition – getting them in the door the first time. We spend more on customer retention. Once they're here we involve them. The airshow pilot gives a lecture after each performance discussing the finer points of his flight. He shakes hands and poses for pictures.

Transient pilots are invited to take to the podium and talk about their airplane, their flying history and what flying has meant to them. Our non-flying guests are encouraged to ask questions. The whole thing is webcast daily from each of our restaurants to our virtual followers.

Food and wine lectures, demonstrations and tastings are held weekly. Ground schools are taught. Aircraft manufacturers are invited to show off their products.

Every month we organize Young Eagle flights with the local EAA chapter. We do low cost catering for local club and charity events. We encourage local civic clubs to hold their meetings on our premises. We support Meals on Wheels and see to it that all of our left offer food finds its way to the needy within our communities.

We are constantly on social media to remind people that lunch is being served or that our airshow is about to start or to show them a picture of a pecan pie fresh out of the oven. We've build a bleacher for people to sit in when they're not joining us for lunch.

The two biggest cards in our marketing deck are couponing and our ears. We listen and we reward customer loyalty. All complaints come to me and I deal with each of them personally. Phone calls are cheap. Sometimes people just need to vent.

"What's next?"

"We now have a recipe that succeeds wherever we take it and we are able to duplicate it at will. I thought that our chickenfried steak menu might limit us to the south but that has not been the case. As you know we currently have 27 restaurants. What you don't know is that we will double that number this year and double it again in each of the following two years."

"Then what?"

"We'll cash out?"

"How?"

"I will not sell to another restaurant operator. We owe our customers more than that. A big restaurant company would move quickly to cut costs and raise profits. That approach would ruin the quality of our product and service. That must never happen. So I'm left with one alternative. We'll go public, we'll IPO!"

"Why raise that much money and take on the grief of quarterly shareholder reports?"

"It's a big world filled with hungry people. There are 15,000 airports in the USA. We intend to have a presence at 10% of them. Cash is king in that play book. Plus I am strongly considering an alternative theme."

"Really? What?"

"Stay tuned."

Who Done It?

Milton's phone rang before his day had officially begun. It was hard to see who was calling without his glasses. He stared hard enough and long enough to see that it was Pastor Dave Holman.

"Hey Dave, I see your up with the chickens."

"The chickens and I have been up for a couple of hours. You gotta' give up that LA time clock you're on and get with our country program.

I need you."

"You've got me. What shall I do and when shall I do it?"

"I need to be in College Station, just across the road from Easterwood Field this evening."

"I heard something about that. Aren't you doing a debate with some hot shot science guy?"

"That's right. You are my high speed transportation department. I have to be there by seven but I can't leave until six fifteen. Can that magic carpet of yours get me where I need to be when I need to be there, yes or no?"

"Yes but……. You need to be at the airport no later than 6:25PM. I'll be in the plane with the engine running."

"I'll be there. See 'ya."

Some pilots have trouble starting the fuel injected engine of the Cherokee 300. Milton never did and this evening was no exception. He lit the fire and it burned. The Cherokee that was now his had been owned by seven others. One of them who had more money than sense had added an air conditioner. In the heat of central Texas Milton was grateful for its presence. By the time

Pastor Dave climbed aboard, things would be on the chilly side. For now it was a sweatbox.

Dave was a punctual preacher. He arrived just as Milton finished setting up his 430's. No reason to file or talk to air traffic control at all. He would fly straight to Easterwood and give them a shout from 10 miles out.

He did most of his final run-up on the roll down the taxi way for runway 34.

"La Grange area traffic Cherokee 785 Charlie Romeo taking the active for immediate takeoff."

Any Cherokee needs flaps for takeoff. Milton brought a special twist. He left the flaps in the neutral position as he rolled down the runway. This reduced drag and allowed the ship to build-up speed quickly. As he passed the speed of rotation, he didn't. Instead he dropped in one notch of flaps and held on. His big Cherokee never disappointed, it always leapt into the sky. He then pushed the yoke forward to stay low and level as his airspeed built. Finally he'd pull back gently and let the beast climb like a rocket.

"La Grange area traffic Piper 785 Charlie Romeo will be a right turn out."

He then turned from the runway heading of 340 degrees to his on course heading of 20 degrees. He'd waste no time climbing as the trip would take no longer than 20 minutes. Two thousand feet seemed about right.

"You good Dave?"

"Yes sir captain. I am strapped in and good to go."

Dave had been to jump school when they were in the Marine Corps together. He was a fearless man as well as a righteous preacher.

"Easterwood Field Piper 785 Charlie Romeo is inbound with information Oscar."

"785 Charlie Romeo report airport in sight."

"Easterwood, 785 Charlie Romeo has the airport in sight."

"785 Charlie Romeo follow the Bonanza on a three mile final for 34."

"Easterwood, 785 Charlie Romeo has the traffic."

"785 Charlie Romeo is cleared to land."

"Cleared to land"

"785 Charlie Romeo take the next turnoff and contact ground point nine."

"Easterwood ground, 785 Charlie Romeo off 34 for the terminal."

"785 Charlie Romeo cleared taxiway Alpha to Lima to the ramp."

"785 Charlie Romeo thank you sir."

The lineman guided them to a tiedown on a very crowded ramp.

"Looks like a lot of folks have flown in to hear you Dave."

"The more the merrier.

I think that long black limousine is for me. Want a lift to the auditorium?"

"Heck yeah, can you get me in."

"Yes sir."

Police cars were everywhere as were poster carting protestors. It wasn't Dave they didn't like it was the message that he was bringing.

Four minutes later they were exiting the big car at the front entrance of the auditorium. Security guards quickly surrounded Dave and Milton and whisked them to the safety of the lobby. Dave was taken away to a dressing room and Milton was escorted to the aisle seat on the very last row. They told him that it would make extracting him safer if required.

The house lights flashed three times and then faded all the way to black. The auditorium was as dark as the blackest starless night imaginable. The rustle of the crowd ceased, became a whisper and reasserted itself.

Eventually, a single beam of light coming from above, behind and beyond the audience focused on a chair in which a man with a kind face, dancing eyes and a laughing smile sat motionless. Once again silence enveloped the audience as Dr. David Holman began to speak without rising from his chair.

"This gathering has been advertised as a debate.

It won't be.

I agree with Professor Charles Stanhope on all of the important 'when', 'where' and 'what' points. Even the 'how' gets no argument from me.

Hopefully you agree as well. Most educated people do as do most religious people like me. It's hard to argue with facts.

Dinosaurs are a great example. We've got their bones and from them have pieced together a pretty good concept of what they looked like.

But the big questions aren't 'when', 'where', 'what' or 'how'. The big questions are 'who' and the real head scratcher 'why'.

Who done it and why did he bother?

How does it all fit together? That is the puzzle we're going to explore this evening?

Our current understanding is that the universe as we know and understand it began with a Big Bang many, many years ago. Charles Stanhope places the date of that event at some 13,700,000 years ago. Let's assume that he is correct as 'when' doesn't matter much anyway.

Charles and many others conjecture about what probably happened on that day that proceeded all other days but they have no theory at all as to the prior state of things.

I find that strange don't you?

What blew up?

Until 1964 every scientist worth his salt professed a belief in a "solid state" universe. They declared that the universe had always existed in its current state and expected that it always would. The majority had held that view for over 2,500 years.

Theologians like me disagreed. We believed then and now in these words. 'In The beginning God created the heavens and the earth.'

It didn't exist and then suddenly it did. That's what we have always held. Call it a Big Bang if you like. I'm not offended by nomenclature.

We, theologians, have waited a long time to welcome Dr. Stanhope and his colleagues to join our belief.

Now for my personal point of view:

No giant rock blew up.

The process was more complex than that. It is best for me to think of it as a shift from the infinite to the finite. There was no matter then there was suddenly all the matter of the universe.

How can that be?

What exactly happened when God created the universe?

I don't know as the Bible, which I consider to be God's word on the subject, doesn't tell us.

God did give us wonderful minds and a large dose of intuition and imagination to ponder the way things are in the physical world and to try to unravel the many mysteries surrounding us. That is our God given nature.

It might be productive to take a moment to deal with the world's most famous equation, $E=MC^2$. We understand this equation to be the genesis of our ability to create atomic explosions and build nuclear reactors.

The amount of energy, E, released is equal to the mass, M, of the material involved times the universal constant, C, squared. The universal constant is the speed of light. That number is approximately, 186,000,000 miles per second. So, a very small amount of material yields a tremendous amount of energy when caused to explode.

To understand what happened on the universe's birthday we need merely take a look at the same equation reversed. $M=E/C^2$. This shows us that it would take a huge amount of energy to make the smallest grain of sand and an unimaginable amount of energy to create all the matter of the universe.

Wouldn't it?

The reversal of the equation $E=MC^2$ solves the riddle of something out of nothing if you accept as I do that matter can be transformed into energy or energy into matter because they are merely two different states of the same think. Like ice and water.

So no 'thing' went bang at all. There was no large rock that suddenly went bang. Instead an enormous amount of energy was transformed.

But that is merely my guess.

What do we know for sure?

First, we know that there is a universe.

We don't know how old it is as we don't know exactly how it was created and from what it was formed.

Let me explain.

The age of the universe in general and the earth in particular is measured using the most precise techniques that the best scientific minds of our age can come up with. They arrive at 13,700,000 years.

The problem is that if you don't know how a thing was made or from what it was made you can't really know its age.

'Outcome' does not reveal 'process' or 'origin' or 'time' only 'outcome'.

We can speculate but we can't possibly know. The material used and the process it was subjected to matters greatly.

Let's examine a simple pot of tea to grasp the significance of what I am suggesting.

A waiter sets a pot of hot water for tea before you.

You cannot know how long it took to raise the temperature of the water in the pot to 212 degrees F simply by measuring the current temperature of the water in the pot. Truth be told you can't even know from what it was made.

What temperature was the water at when the process started?

Was water used or did the experiment begin by combining hydrogen and oxygen?

Was it brought to a boil on an electric stove top, or on a gas stove or in a microwave oven? Perhaps it came from an instant hot water faucet.

The time it took to boil the water could vary from twenty minutes to less than a second, couldn't it?

The point is that to know the age of anything, the earth included, you must know a great deal about how it was created and from what it was created. A simple measure of temperature or the decay of carbon 14 molecules can't supply the answer.

Not convinced?

Let's discuss carbon in general, diamonds in particular. If I give you a handful of flawless diamonds and ask their age, an incorrect assumption will cause your answer to be off by millions of years. Diamonds are formed deep within the earth's crust over millions of years, we think.

That could be but………..

Diamonds of equal quality to natural ones are made by man in less than a day.

The man made ones are so good that even an expert cannot discern the difference between natural and man-made. So we can't know the length of time required to create a diamond by merely examining the diamond.

Actually, it is not possible to know the age of anything without knowing the process and the materials used to create it. Was the boiling water we discussed earlier initially at 210 degrees F or 0 degrees F before it was placed on the burner? That would make a difference wouldn't it?

We'll talk a lot this afternoon about what happened and when it happened, how it happened and even where it happened. But this is not a story about those questions.

'In the beginning God created the heavens and the earth.'

This is a 'who' and 'why' story.

This is a 'who done it' and as importantly 'why'.

Now help me to welcome my dear friend, Professor Charles Stanhope, our nation's most heralded theoretical physicist and my friend for more than thirty years."

The applause was loud and many, indeed most of the audience stood, for they had come to hear Professor Charles Stanhope. They had seen his television specials on PBS and they had bought his books. Now they would see him in person and a lucky few would actually meet him and shake his hand.

Dr. Stanhope came on stage, walked first to Dave Holman, smiled broadly, shook his hand warmly and moved directly to the lectern. Before he could utter a word, the crowd once more broke into thunderous applause. The rail thin champion of science raised both arms above his six foot four inch stature and motioned his thanks to the crowd. Seemingly, he had won this debate before it had even begun.

Finally, the clapping subsided and Charles Stanhope began.

"Dave began by saying there would be no debate here tonight as he agreed with everything I believe in. Then point by point he attacked the basic premises of my beliefs.

Let me start in much the same way by exploring Dave's principal precept.

'In The beginning God created the heavens and the earth.'

Dave believes that because it is written in his Bible. In fact it is the first line of his Bible. There are many books in the Bible and none is more important than the first one; Genesis. Here the tone and texture is set. So let's explore this creation fable for a couple of minutes and see whether we should believe it or dismiss it.

Nowhere does it say when God created the heavens and earth exactly. The date isn't given or even hinted at. God doesn't tell us but he does as Dr. Holman points out give us good minds to use to find the answer to this riddle.

How are we to do that?

Fortunately we don't have to as Bishop James Usher, a 17th-century Irish cleric did it for us. He calculated that creation occurred in 4004 B.C. by using Biblical chronology. Who was whose father? That information is provided in the Bible all the way back to Adam. There were many such estimates, provided by other Biblical Scholars. While they differ a bit as to the exact date of creation, each results in the Earth and the Universe being approximately 6,000 years old.

Well a lot happened in 6,000 years didn't it? Let's explore a couple of them. Dinosaurs came into existence, flourished and became extinct. There are no reports of anyone seeing a dinosaur in the Middle East during the last 6,000 years. Nor are there such reports or cave drawings in China, Europe, Africa, Australia or America. None, none at all. No human being ever chronicled an encounter with a dinosaur. How can that be?

I know what we should do. Let's ask the expert on the Bible. Let's ask Dr. Holman.

Dave can you help us out on this point?"

"Absolutely, I am grateful that you asked!

Charles is correct when he says that the Bible is divided into books and that the first book is Genesis.

Each book is divided into Chapters and each Chapter into Verses. That division allows us to keep things in order.

Genesis I deals with the first six days of creation. It informs us generally what God created on each of those days. On the sixth day, the last day mentioned in Chapter I, God created mankind.

In Genesis II, God observed that the creation was complete and so He rested on the seventh day. Following that day, we are told in the 7th verse that God formed a man from dust, called him Adam and placed him in the Garden of Eden.

Pay close attention to what we are told and what we are not told. We know simply that God created mankind before He created Adam. That is how the Bible lays it out. Further it gives us no details as to how much time passed between the creation of mankind and the creation of Adam. Therefore, calculating the date of the creation of Adam, even if correct, informs us not at all about the age of man and certainly tells us nothing about the age of the universe.

I could go on but Charles was generous to call on me and I don't want to misuse that kindness."

"Well David that was very, very well done. I am puzzled by the first chapter and the days. Were they ordinary twenty four hour days or were they of unusual length and what was that length if you know?"

"The Bible proclaims that the first seven days were 24 hours long just as all the days that followed them are. But let's be clear that the days don't begin until after the earth was formed. The first paragraph of Chapter I says:

'*In the beginning God created the heavens and the earth. Now the earth was formless and empty, darkness was over the surface of the deep, and the Spirit of God was hovering over the waters.*'

Then it goes to the first day beginning with verse three:

'And God said, "Let there be light," and there was light. God saw that the light was good, and He separated the light from the darkness. God called the light "day," and the darkness He called "night." And there was evening, and there was morning—the first day.'

To my mind that's a 24 hour day. Just like yesterday and hopefully today.

But Charles, be careful not to judge just how much God can do in a 24 hour day. I would speculate that it is a good deal more than we can do. Nor should we imagine what process He used to do what He did. Could God cause evolution to occur at a faster rate than it might have proceeded without His intervention? My answer is certainly He can, just as I can boil a pot of water more quickly in a microwave oven than I can on a stove top. His ways are different than our ways Charles."

Just then the lights of the auditorium came on and seven Texas State Troopers walked onto the stage. They approached the two shocked men who were now frozen in the middle of the stage.

The Trooper who appeared to be in charge spoke these chilling words, "Dr. David Holman you are a person of interest in the homicide investigation of Mr. Leon Greenfeldt. We are placing you under arrest as part of that investigation and for your own protection. Please place your hands behind you."

Dr. David Holman was handcuffed and escorted off the stage under very heavy security.

Dr. Charles Stanhope said, "I am sure there is some mistake. I know this man well. He could not possibly be involved in a homicide.

Where are you taking him?"

"We can't say at this time. Please stand aside sir."

Dr. Stanhope moved aside and said, "David, I'll get my personal lawyer on this immediately."

From the back of the auditorium Milton Muzny saw what had just taken place and heard those words, "homicide investigation of Mr. Leon Greenfeldt."

Homicide of Leon Greenfeldt? Made no sense, no sense at all.
Milton needed to get out of here quietly and quickly. He couldn't
help David if he also was in jail and if they were arresting David
they must be looking for him as well.

He could see that all of the exit doors were manned by State
Troopers and that everyone was being questioned as they left.
Milton bolted up the side stairs of the auditorium to the balcony.
From there he made his way into the AV room and onto the
catwalks where the spot lights were nested. Then he did the only
thing he could do, remain motionless for the three hours that it
took for the police to empty the auditorium and exit.

When all of the lights were turned off, silently and slowly he
crawled back to the stairwell and followed it to the door that led to
the roof. He moved as he had been taught too many years ago in
the Marine Corps' Scout Sniper School. It all came back, each step
as slowly taken as the one before, each joint of his body moving
separately, quietly, deliberately. It took time but he had time, what
he needed was a clear escape route.

He reached the fire escape and eventually the ground. Then across
campus and to the fence line of Easterwood Field which separated
him from his Cherokee. He could see it and the Trooper that was
guarding it.

Escape even for the moment wasn't going to be easy if possible at
all. Then a gift came along with his name on it.

Shift change.

The guard on duty walked towards the trooper who was coming on
duty. They laughed and walked together into the terminal.

Coffee break? Too easy on the one hand but gift horses are never
to be looked in the mouth on the other hand.

Over the fence and to his ship in what seemed like a single bound.
This flight would be made without a preflight, a run up or the
nicety of a runway.

Milton fired-up the Cherokee and headed for the taxiway. The terminal door opened as he did. Two troopers dropped two hot coffees and grabbed pistols from their holsters. Shoots would soon be fired his way. No doubt about that.

The skin of an airplane is slightly thicker than tissue paper which makes it light but definitely not armor platted. The strength comes for the stringers and spars, everything else is window dressing.

The bullets came as he made the turn from the ramp to the taxiway. Some whizzed by others bounced off the concrete and one or two ripped through 785 Charlie Romeo's aluminum skin. Near as he could tell none had hit him, at least not yet. Throttle forward, body down, off to the races he went.

Milton yanked the Cherokee into the air before it was ready to fly. That was his intention. If he could get it into ground effect it would pick up speed more quickly.

Soon he was floating on a cushion of air and waiting for airspeed to build as he grasped his way out of bullet range. The airspeed built quickly now. He could easily climb but he decided to stay at five feet and build up a head of steam. Soon he was moving along at 110 knots and nearing the airport's perimeter fence. He pulled up slightly just enough to clear the trees.

His plan was simple, stay below radar and get to the river. Once there he could fly along below the edge of the Brazos River's banks undetected. Following the river north for a while and then he'd jump into the clear blue – transponder off naturally!

Eventually, he'd make a southwest turn and head for the FiveOnFive Ranch just outside Giddings. Few knew that it was his as the name on the deed was M.A. Butler and fewer still knew it had an airstrip. One day he needed to get around to telling the FAA about it but he hadn't yet. Sometimes procrastination pays off.

That's exactly what he did.

At 6,000 feet above the FiveOnFive Ranch he killed the engine and began a circling glide to his grass strip and the relative safety of his hangar which looked like any other pole barn that dotted this country side.

Gliding isn't something that any Cherokee is good at, particularly not the 300. They are the result of an unholy breeding of a dove with a brick. When under power they fly very well, cut the engine and the other side of their lineage brakes through. The only way to win is to make the ship believe it still had power by keeping the airspeed up which was easy to do in a more than shallow dive. That's why he went to 6,000 to start his approach.

He pointed down and made turns of the circle steep. Airspeed remained at a planned 105 knots. If it fell off Milton steepened the dive if it got too hot he pulled back. One hundred and five was just what the doctor ordered. He had actually planned and executed this approach many times. 1000 feet from his fence he needed to be 800 feet above his neighbor's ranch. Then he would execute an extreme slip to dump altitude all the way down to 40 feet as he crossed his fence line.

785 Charlie Romeo's tires kissed the dew laden grass of FiveOnFive's secret turf strip. If you didn't know it was here, you'd never be able to pick it out from the air.

In the glove box was a standard garage door opener that signaled a heavy duty motor to unlatch and swing open the entire side of his pole barn. No one would believe it was a hangar unless you saw an airplane inside.

The setup hadn't been created to avoid law enforcement. It was all about hiding his FiveOnFive development center. He flew here every day after the restaurant office closed to tweak his golf clubs as he tried to find the right formula. It had taken two years. The turf strip doubled as a driving range. Now they were ready for the US Open Championship. Quietly he had assembled a team for his assault on the Open. The goal was to get a lot of TV time and to win. It was possible even if not probable.

So now what? Milton was on the ground and in his hangar. He was safe for a while but he was also a fugitive wanted in connection with a murder or at least that's what he imagined. The bullets fired at him affirmed his belief.

From the barn, he started making calls to Eddie Ray using his landline not his cell phone which he had thrown away back at Easterwood Field.

No answer.

Eddie Ray had turtled on the world or at least Milton.

He mashed the right buttons to make Reba's phone ring. She quickly answered.

"Reba, its Milton."

"What have you done? The police are everywhere looking for you."

"I have no idea. They detained David Holman as I watched from the audience at last night's debate. If they wanted him they must be really anxious to get me but I can't figure out why.

Leon Greenfeldt died of natural causes in a hospital in Los Angeles."

"That's not what the police think, Milton. They dug him up this afternoon and found a hole in his skull made by a .357.

Sounds like murder, wouldn't you say?"

"Heck yeah, I'd have to go along with their theory on that one. Any idea where Eddie Ray is?"

"I know they're looking for him all over the country. It looks like they have him as the murderer and you and David as accomplices."

"Reba, I never even met Leon Greenfeldt while he was alive and couldn't pick him out of a crowd if he still walked among us. All I know is that he was a friend of Eddie Ray's."

"The police say he was actually a partner in a business deal that went south. They theorize that Eddie Ray felt cheated, maybe he was, and sought revenge. People do that you know?"

"Yes I do.

As a matter of fact if I could get my hands on Eddie Ray right now there could be another murder for the police to investigate."

"What do you intend to do?"

"Well, I was trying to get in touch with Eddie Ray to figure out what's going on. My next call will be to my attorney, 'Cool' Guy Smyrle. I need to turn myself in and I'd like to have him there when I do it."

"Makes sense."

"Bye for now. Wish me luck."

"Good Luck."

Reba hung up and smiled disgustedly at Lt. Mitch Thackery who had listened in on the whole telephone conversation. Milton should have realized that the police would head for Reba's place. He was tired and he just made his first mistake.

"Guy? It's Milton."

"I figured you'd be calling. You're in a pretty big mess right now son."

"I know. Help me get out of it."

"It will be expensive. I'll need 40K upfront."

"Call Reba. She'll get it to you."

"Cash Milton."

"OK cash. Now how do we get me turned in and can we keep me out of jail?

"Step one will be easy, step two not so much. I need to get hold of the District Attorney for Fayette County, Ronnie Earle, to set it up."

"Fayette County? I figured the State of California was the one pushing this thing."

"They are. California wants you on the murder charge. If I can get Fayette County to arrest you on any sort of felony charge then California will have to wait in line and we can keep you here while we sort things out."

"Work your magic."

"I will but Milton, I mean cash and I mean upfront."

"Call Reba."

"Fine, meet me at my office at 1 PM."

"No. I'll meet you at 1 PM but not at your office."

"Paranoia kicking in, son?"

"Big time!"

"Good, it should be. Call me and let me know where and when and use a burner."

"What's a burner?"

"Milton for a felon on the run you've got a lot to learn. Go to a drug store and buy a prepaid phone. Do it with cash. Burn the phone every day and get a new one. Just so we're clear burn the phone means to throw it away."

"Being a criminal on the run gets expensive doesn't it?"

"It does Milton, it surely does."

Four

Long days passed and turned into long weeks as Guy Smyrle did his job of keeping Milton in Texas and out of jail. Guy was good and made it look easy. Milton was charged with participating in a criminal conspiracy to defraud Leon Greenfeldt's estate. California's Attorney General couldn't believe that his staff had been out flanked by a small town Texas attorney and promised to arrest and charge Milton with murder if he showed up in California.

Guy used Milton's money to hire a private detective to track down Eddie Ray Farrell.

"Milton, you're out for now and this deal will probably go away if we can prove the story you're telling is true. The easiest way to do that is to grab Eddie Ray before they do. It looks like somebody shot Leon and Eddie Ray is a pretty good candidate. We don't want him going 'wormy' on us and cutting a deal with the prosecutor who is mad as a hornet at us right now. It wouldn't be the first time I've seen the trigger man walk and the wheel man go to the big house. Sometimes, Lady Justice isn't just blind she's drunk." Guy loved to lecture his clients. Their money wasn't enough he wanted them to feel beholden.

"Guy, I have no idea where Eddie Ray is but I think I know how to smoke him out?" Milton spoke evenly, like a man who didn't have a care in the world.

"How's that Milton?" Guy leaned forward.

"He loaned me some money when I was starting the **Chickenfried Café**."

Guy interrupted, "Would that be the $200,000 in cash that you gave to Reba which she deposited into your account at her Daddy's bank?"

"It would."

"California's trying to pull rabbits out of hats to get that money back. They say it came from Leon's safe in his office in Redondo Beach."

"That could be, but it could also have come from somewhere else. I don't know about that. I asked Eddie Ray for a loan and he UPSed it to me. The deal called for me to UPS $5,000 a month in cash back to him each month until the debt was repaid. I've been doing that.

The address he asks me to use changes every other month or so. This month it is to go to a Berth B223 at the Redondo Beach Yacht Harbor. I assume Eddie Ray has a boat."

"How interesting. I'll get my girl right on it."

"Girl? What girl?"

"The private investigator I hired for you is a girl, a very hot girl who has no trouble gaining access to pretty much anywhere. A yacht harbor should be a piece of cake."

"Guy, you're a real piece of work.

What should I do now? Do I have to stay in Texas?"

"No just stay connected to me and stay out of California."

"Great I've got a business to run and more restaurants to open."

"Go to it son. You need to make money cause I'm gonna' need it to keep you out of jail."

 "Can we talk about FiveOnFive?" Milton's story was getting longer than Angela's deadline

"Sure."

"Twenty-three players swinging your FiveOnFive clubs advanced from the 111 local qualifying rounds for the US Open to the 12 sectionals. Did you know about that in advance?" Angela was anxious to get something she could turn into a Sports Illustrated article.

"Of course, I did. The only way to get a set of FiveOnFive's at that time was to have me give them to you. Everyone that had a set got them directly from me as a gift."

"10,000 golfers from around the world entered the locals for their shot at one of the 156 US Open playing positions; about 1,200 are still in the hunt and have moved onto the sectionals. Two to three players from each of the sectionals will be invited to compete at Pinehurst #2 for the US Open title. What's your goal? Why have you equipped these twenty-three unknown players?"

"First of all, they're not complete unknowns. Their mother's know and love each one of them. My goal is simply to have FiveOnFives in the winner's bag."

"Is that even possible?"

"Possible? No.

Probable? Yes!

We're gonna' win this thing for two simple reasons. We have the best equipment and the best players."

"That's brash!"

"No that's honest. Not a single exempt player heading to the US Open has a 'fairways made' percentage above 70. Not a single one of my guys had a 'fairways made' percentage lower than 100 during the local qualifying rounds.

Let that sink in for a moment.

The FiveOnFive Staff played perfect golf off the tee. They didn't put a single ball into the rough, out-of-bounds, a watertrap or a fairway bunker. They kept their ball in play.

There are three statistics I care about: fairways made in regulation, greens hit in regulations and greens putted in regulation. Against that measure our Staff played perfect golf. No one missed a fairway and everyone reached every green in regulation. No one took more than two putts on any green.

That translates into score cards showing pars and birdies exclusively; no bogies, no double bogies on the one hand and no eagles on the other. My Staff play a disciplined game, simple has that."

"Milton, everything you say is true. I have studied their stats, which brings up a couple of questions. Your guys are not long ball hitters. They average 250 yards off the tee with the big stick. The leading pros on the tour are beating that by almost 100 yards. How can you expect your guys to compete?"

"Easy. Winning golf isn't about distance, that's a fallacy. It's about accuracy. Those guys you mentioned do drive 320 yards or so. The problem is they have distance but no control. Sometimes they go 320 yards down the fairway mostly they go 320 yards into the rough. How does that help? I'll answer my own question, it doesn't.

Here's the big difference between my sticks and every other manufacturer's, with theirs' the distance the ball travels varies based on the guy that swings the club. Our clubs are designed for the ball to travel a very specific distance no matter who swings the club. In the case of my driver, its 250 yards, period. The distance the ball travels when hit with one of our clubs varies based on the club selected not the player selecting it. If you pick up my driver and slam a tee shot 320 yards it isn't because you're good; on the contrary, it is because you hit the ball poorly. My driver is setup to move the ball exactly 250 yards. Golf is not about muscle power, it's about brain power."

"Milton, I'm having trouble understanding how that can be so. Can you help me out?"

"Sure. It goes to the long version of my company's name. It is **Five On Five In**. Meaning every club is designed exactly like a five iron so every swing you take is a five iron swing which is the easiest swing to teach and to learn. So you use the **Five** to get **On** the green. Once on the green, **Five** takes on a new meaning. My putter looks more like a mallet than a blade. Hence you must strike the ball precisely, that makes it go straight which is the strategy my clubs are built on. Our **FREE** YouTube video series on BIG Hole putting is available to everyone not just my future customers. It teaches BIG Hole putting. We talked about this once before didn't we?"

"Yes, could you walk me through it again?"

"The important thing is to imagine a ten foot diameter cup rather than a 4 inch diameter one. Your first putt from anywhere on the green must stop inside the 10 foot imaginary cup. That's pretty easy to consider but it is very hard to do and requires practice. Eventually though everyone who adopts the BIG Hole putting strategy gets there. The reward is that the first putt no matter how long it is winds up a maximum of five feet away from the four inch cup. There's that number five again. Our Staff players spend three hours a day sinking five foot putts every day of their lives. When they are within five feet of the cup the ball drops 100% of the time. It isn't that they are each that good. It is that they practice that much. Someday soon, our customers will have the same experience. First, we'll sell them the right tool, and then we'll teach them how to use it. We'll succeed because they'll succeed, that's our strategy. Successful customers translate into a successful company. Half the strokes on every golf course occur on the putting green."

"Par shooters don't win golf tournaments. You have to be under par to win."

"If you can count on shooting par on every round you'll be in contention at every tournament. Then it's a matter of reaching the green in less than regulation or getting the ball within five feet of the cup with your approach shot or sinking your first putt even if it's longer than five feet away.

Getting on the green in less than regulation is unlikely for our players. We can never drive a par four hole given our 250 yard criteria and we aren't likely to reach a par five with two strokes for a similar reason. However, accurate aim and precise club performance occasionally allows us to put an approach shot within five feet of the cup. Sinking putts from further away than five feet is also not in our wheelhouse. We practice five foot putts not ten or fifteen foot putts. The difference is huge. Here's why.

Putting involves proper aim, precise power and accurate distance. Of the three, distance is the most important. The further you are from the cup the more important aim and power become as they must compensate for the speed and break of the green. 'Reading' a green is a black art similar to fortune telling. It is more about the happenstance of a green leaning in the proper direction at the proper slope with the proper green speed for the golfer to adjust his aim and power to overcome gravity by a precise amount. When it happens it is thrilling to watch because it is such a measure of luck. My Staff is trained to yield to skill and abandon the randomness of luck. Within five feet, the influence of break and green speed are largely diminished. Because five feet is the sweet spot of the green our entire attention is focused on getting within five feet with the approach shot or first putt. If it happens with the first putt we see a par. If it happens with the approach shot then we see a birdie."

"How many birdies do your players get per round?"

"That goes to the third leg of our stool, golf course intelligence and round preparation. You can't expect the magic of a birdie to happen on your first visit to a course that you know nothing about. Golf is a contest between each player and the course not between players.

We study the course using satellite photos and geodetic maps. They allow us to fill our course notebook with distances and landing zones. We demand that every tee shot on a par four or five land in the fairway. If we're using our driver that means in the fairway 250 yards from the tee. Varying the distance of the tee shot can't happen with my clubs but the tee location on the tee box can vary by a few yards to the left or right or to the rear. That's important and the landing zone selected can be anywhere between the boundaries of the fairway. So if we are dealing with a dog leg to the left that occurs 220 yards down the fairway our pick would be a drive down the left side of the fairway from the left side of the tee box. Our ball will then be a few yards closer to the green than if we had targeted the fairway's exact center.

Golf is like billiards, every shot must set up the next shot. Therefore, the distance and position from the tee is important but the landing zone of the tee shot must be the most favorable place for approaching the green. In our previous example being a few yards closer to the green would not be the wise choice if it left you facing a sandtrap.

Much is learned from mapping but there is no substitute for studying the course by walking, measuring and photographing it especially the greens. Then and only then do we play practice rounds, many, many practice rounds, beating the course demands knowing the course."

"When did you start developing the clubs?"

"When I was living Rancho Santa Fe. I had closed out my career in the computer business and was casting around for something to do. During those days I played a lot of golf and became frustrated by the game rather than pleasured by it. Soon I was struck that many others must feel the same way. Golf is way harder to play than it needs to be. The concept of a right sized golf club came to me and never left though I didn't do anything about it until I came to La Grange.

Quickly I learned that merely making all the clubs the same length wasn't enough. I needed to rebalance each of them and change all of their lofts. That worked but I was left with clubs that went erratic distances, the five iron would carry further than the four iron. The design process required much more thought. Finally it hit me that I should first determine the performance I wanted from each club and then tweak until I got it. Here are my design goals in yards per club:

Driver 250
3-wood 230
4-wood 220
2-iron 190
3-iron 180
4-iron 170
5-iron 160
6-iron 140
7-iron 120
8-iron 110
9-iron 100
PW 90
SW 70

It's amazing how much easier the process became when I had a set goal, club heads could be reweighted, face lofts changed, shafts stiffened or relaxed until the club had the right feel and the performance equaled the goal. While I was at it, the circumferences of the club handles were increased until they became comfortable. The interlocking grip is a silly attempt to make your hands deal with an object ill-suited for them. I fixed that problem."

"So what grip do you use?"

"Baseball, as our handles are equal to those of a baseball bat. It's comfortable and secure.

The first thing golfers notice about our sticks is their length. The second is that the shafts are square not round."

"What materials do you use?"

"The clubs are one piece, shaft, head and handle. They are molded from carbon fiber. Given the lightness and strength of the material weights must be added during the molding process. It took a while to figure out the precise weight to place in each club head but I eventually got there.

One more thing, they are fire-engine red from top to bottom. The grips are wrapped with white perforated leather.

Because the clubs are different the bag was designed to reflect and compensate. It is crafted from a rich, tan leather into a thin rectangle. Each club has its own molded and lined pocket. They are arrayed in five rows of three pockets each. An umbrella occupies the extra one. Lidded storage compartments replace the zippered pockets of the previous century's bags. A pair of bag length legs can be extended from one side of the bag to hold it in a slightly tilted upright fashion when set down. The bag is the answer to every caddie's unspoken prayer."

"Why the US Open?"

"As its name implies it is open. I wanted my Staff to be unknowns not celebrities. Two years ago I began recruiting them. The idea was to enlist young guys who wanted to be touring pros but hadn't made the cut. All had college golf team experience and all were good but none were standouts."

"How many? I know that twenty three have advanced to the sectionals but how many did you enter?"

"Twenty five, one got sick and had to withdraw the other was arrested the night before his tournament. Domestic Violence I think."

"What has all of this cost you?"

"Very little to this point, I sponsor each guy which means I cover his traveling and training expenses and provide his equipment and clothing. They keep 100% of their winnings but must stick with me for five years. I can and will drop them if they don't qualify for the Open. They get $100,000 if they do and another $100,000 if they make the cut. That's pretty much the contract and the deal."

"How many do you think have a real chance?"

"Three to five of them will qualify. All that qualify will make the cut."

"I expected you to say twenty-three."

"Angela, I'm egotistical but I'm also a realist. The sectionals are loaded with very good players. Only two or three guys move up from each of those twelve contests. My guys will play very well, I have no doubt about that but so will the others. At the end of the day it goes to the players with the lowest scores. We're tweaked towards par. So we'll have to get mighty lucky at a time that everybody else gets snake bit.

We've got a good chance but only a chance. We'll see what we see."

"Have you been contacted yet by the media about your presence?"

"Only you."

"Why's that?"

"I don't know really. I suspect that it has a lot to do with your bloodhound reporter skills. You smoked me out."

"No, I didn't. This was an assignment. I was told to contact you."

"Interesting."

"One more question. Where did you get the money?"

"California is a target rich environment for angel investors. I know many of them as a result of my days in the computer business. Several of the ones who play golf were anxious to pony up."

"You're a charmed man Milton Muzny."

"I know."

It was late so they left it there. Angela went to her RV. Milton called Reba for a nightcap.

Two weeks later, FiveOnFive's bank account was half a million dollars poorer as five of the guys qualified.

A NetJets flight touched down in La Grange with the five US Open sectional winners onboard. Five grinning, grateful faces attached to five young men who were each very, very grateful for the change Milton had brought to their lives.

Jean-François had planned a special dinner to be served on the rooftop. Charcoaled steaks, baked potatoes, tossed green salad, homemade vanilla ice cream and pecan pie. This was a dinner for American golfers. Kentucky bourbon was substituted for the French wine Jean-François would have preferred serving.

The dinner was loud, congratulatory and fun. As the dessert forks hit empty plates almost in unison, the sky lit up with fireworks launched from the other side of the field. The show went on for thirty minutes at least. It was a jaw dropping end to a great dinner.

"Men, you've made me proud. Reba, pass out the cash."

Reba handed each of the players a small red leather duffle bag with the FiveOnFive logo emblazoned in gold on its side. Each held one hundred thousand dollars' worth of Benjamin's.

Smiles all around.

"Gentlemen, I'll see you in two weeks at Pinehurst #2. The jet will be here in fifteen minutes to take you there. Your job is to spend every minute of the next two weeks figuring out the course. Getting the condition and feel of the greens into your bones is going to be critical. Work together, teach each other, share now, when the tournament starts you can rip each other's throats out, for now be friends.

Make me proud."

The jet blasted into the dark skies and Milton wondered out loud, "When will the phone ring?"

Reba was surprised, "Doesn't your phone ring enough? Who are you expecting to call?"

"Reba, soon this apron will be filled with sports writers. FiveOnFive is an amazing story. I am shocked that they have not discovered it yet. But they will."

"Why do you want that to happen, ego?"

"Gosh no. Money, it's all about money. FiveOnFive is the first new golf club manufacturer in many years and the only one in the history of golf that makes the game approachable by the average Joe. Sometime during the US Open we should be overwhelmed with orders."

"Really? Now that is your ego talking. You don't have two big things that you surely need; a factory to build your clubs and stores to sell them. So if somebody wants a set, you don't have any and if you did they can't buy them anywhere."

"Wrong on both counts Baby Girl. I've setup two pilot manufacturing shops, one for the clubs in Kerrville and the other for the bags in El Paso. All sales will be made factory direct on the FiveOnFive website which will go live on the first day of the US Open."

"It's the first I'm hearing about it."

"Milton Muzny 'International Man of Mystery', Baby Girl you don't know nearly as much about me as you think you do."

"Don't I know it, but tell me this much. Don't your clubs have to be made custom for each player?"

"That's right which is why we sell them factory direct from our website. It tells them where and how to measure their body. Those measurements must be included with each order. The factory is a robotics oriented foundry. An order comes in, the computer calculates the metrics for each club based on those measurements and spits out a finished set. They are then dressed, weighed and tested."

"What's dressed mean?"

"They are sanded and buffed. Then the handle is wrapped. That's pretty much it."

"How are they tested?"

"FiveOnFive has a robot which self-adjusts to the body measurements associated with each club. A ball is auto placed just before the robot takes a swing. The results are sensed, measured and compared against the standard. When an entire set passes quality control it is mated with one of the bags from El Paso, boxed, labeled and shipped.

Simple."

"Milton, why did you set the club manufacturing shop in Kerrville and the bag shop in El Paso? Why not La Grange? We could use the jobs you know."

"I wanted to put everything in La Grange.

Kerrville has a large number of skilled aircraft workers who used to be employed by Mooney Aircraft. Their skills translate easily to our process. The same is true in El Paso with former Justin Boot employees. Each group hits the ground running with our products and processes. A shallow learning curve leads to a quick ramp-up.

As to La Grange, the fulfillment center for the **Chickenfried Chicken Coop** website is here already and will grow steadily. There will soon be many FiveOnFive branded products that will also be stocked and shipped from the La Grange fulfillment center."

"Goodnight Milton. See 'ya in the morning."

"Reba, why don't you spend the night here with me? We could continue the celebration."

"There's a proposal, a ring and ceremony in their someplace, right?"

"Soon there will be."

"See 'ya in the morning."

Milton's world was speeding up. **Chickenfried Café's** business was booming and the chain was expanding. FiveOnFive's launch was going to be rocky and explosive. He knew that the media would discover FiveOnFive over the next two weeks. There would be a great debate about what he was doing and his right to do it. A complete unknown from La Grange, Texas was about to change the world of golf. There would be many who would fight to preserve the status quo and that meant attacking Milton Muzny. Given the criminal charges he was facing with the promise of more to come he was an easy target. Eddie Ray Farrell was really messing up his life plan on the one hand. On the other hand, it was Eddie Ray who had brought Milton back to Texas; the friends he missed and the life he wanted to regain.

Where the heck was Eddie Ray? Would Guy Smyrle's detective lady find him? Would he clear Milton or try to do a deal with the prosecutor? Was Milton destined to become the unsuspecting wheelman who spent the rest of his life in prison for a crime that he didn't even know happened? Sleep eluded Milton.

Deidra Longmuffin checked in with Guy every morning. "Hey Guy, here's the deal I have been able to buy a boat in the adjacent slip to the Eddie Ray's. I got a great deal on a Cal 28. We'll sell it before I head home. For now, let Milton know he's out ten large plus a $350 slip fee. The UPS tracking info you gave me says our box is out for delivery. I'll be sun tanning on our boat's deck when it arrives. Hopefully I can attract Eddie Ray's attention."

"Good work Deidra. Be sure and wear the little red bikini of yours. That should draw him in."

"I'll be in touch."

It was three in the afternoon when the big brown truck showed up. Deidra had made an error and it could be a serious one. The driver made all of his deliveries to the Marina office not to each boat. She saw him go in with a box that looked like theirs stacked on his cart with all the others. He was as efficient as the company that employed him, in and out and back on the road in less than three minutes. She barely had time to put on a shirt and shoes before seeing a man enter the office and leave with her package. His pace picked up as he reached the parking lot and pulled a set of keys from his pocket.

Suddenly her revolver was pressed into the right side of his neck, "Hands up drop to your knees and do it now Eddie Ray." Her tone would have brought a drill instructor to attention.

"I ain't Eddie Ray." he cried.

"And I ain't the tooth fairy.

Now you're going to do exactly what I tell you, when I tell you, the way I tell you or you'll miss breakfast, lunch and dinner from this day forward.

Got it?"

"Yes Ma'am."

"Hands behind you," Deidra cuffed him and pulled his wallet from the back pocket of his jeans.

His driver's license said Roy Simmons and the picture matched her captive.

"Where is he?"

"Who?"

"Don't go stupid on me because if you do you're dead. The name on that box isn't yours clown boy. Where's the guy whose name is on the box?"

"I don't know. I really don't."

"You've got one last chance to give the right answer, so you think about what you're going to say. Three questions and you need the right answer to each of them:

First: Who sent you to pick up this package?
Second: What are you supposed to do with the package?
Third: When are you supposed to have it done?

Now think really hard and give me a set of really good answers so I don't have to cap you?"

"Eddie Ray Farrell is a sailing buddy of mine. He asked me if I'd pick up this package for him and leave it on his boat. He told me it was a new ship-to-shore radio. He said he would be down tonight and would sail to Catalina then. The office would be closed by the time he got here. I live on my boat so it was no problem for me to do him this favor."

"So why didn't you do that?"

"I was going to when you grabbed me. Look in the back seat of my car. Those are groceries that I just bought and was going to carry to my boat which is a few slips down the dock from Milton's."

"Good story, for your sake I hope it's true. I'm going to put the gun away and we're going to walk to Eddie Ray's boat together. If you try anything funny I'll shove you into the water and you'll drown. Swimming with their hands cuffed behind their back isn't something most people can do. You're probably one of them.

Are the keys to his boat in your pocket?"

"Yes."

She slid her long slender fingers into his front right jean's pocket and smiled as she did it. Slowly Deidra extracted them.

"Now you be nice and this may not turn out so badly."

"Yes Ma'am."

"Roy, hold up. Introduce me to your lady friend Bro."

Deidra turned slightly and caught her first glimpse of Eddie Ray Farrell in the flesh. He trotted up behind them and slapped Roy on back as he noticed the handcuffs. Without losing a step he spun Roy and slammed him into Deidra knocking her into the water and grabbing Roy in time to keep him from following her into the drink.

Before she bobbed back to the surface they were gone, Eddie Ray, Roy and the UPS package. In less than a second she had gone from hero to zero.

Milton answered his ringing phone which announced an incoming call from someone in Florida. "You got Milton Muzny. How can I help you?"

"Mr. Muzny this is Ed Herschel with the USGA. I am calling to discuss FiveOnFive. Do I have the right number?"

"Yes Mr. Herschel you do. What's up?"

"Well, Mr. Muzny, you are to be congratulated with the amazing success of the golfers carrying your clubs in our qualifying process. We've never seen anything like the success the players swinging your clubs have enjoyed. I think twenty-three of them topped the leader board at their local qualifying event and five advanced from the sectionals to the tournament. That is very impressive.

The press corps has been pounding me for information on you, your company, your clubs and your players. They want background, pictures and interviews. With your permission, I'll provide them with your name and phone number."

"That'd be fine."

"Excellent! Now for a small problem, Rule #4 of the Rules of Golf requires all manufacturers to submit a sample of their equipment to us for a ruling on its conformity to our rules before they go into production. I can't locate your paperwork or a sample of your equipment. I telephoned my counterpart at the PGA and he claims not to have your submission either or any record of a ruling."

"I see."

"Well Mr. Muzny can you help me out?"

"I'd be pleased to try."

"Terrific. Could you send me a copy of your written submission and your copy of our ruling accepting your clubs? I'm sorry for having to ask but without that ruling I don't see how we can allow your players to compete in our tournament."

"You mean 'continue' to compete in your tournament don't you?" Milton's growing anger flashed in his tone.

"Mr. Muzny, I think that's a distinction without a difference. I'm not your enemy on this though I realize it might seem that way. FiveOnFive and its clubs are on the cusp of making a huge contribution to the game of golf. That said we are governed by a set of well-defined rules which I am charged with enforcing.

The USGA will work with you to fast track your submission if you haven't yet made it and choose to do so now."

"Let me check with my staff to see who made the submission and when that occurred. Are you saying that you have accepted the qualification of my players based on their performance in the locals and the sectionals and that all we're discussing is allowing them to tee off at Pinehurst?"

"Yes that is what I am saying. We are not seeking to nullify their qualifications or disqualify them even if no submission was previously made as long as the submission is made now and the clubs conform.

Mr. Muzny, can we work together to resolve this issue amicably? Will you search your company's records and send me the paperwork I need if it exists. If it doesn't will you make such a submission?"

"How much time do I have?"

"Shall we say seventy-two hours?"

"OK, seventy-hours it is."

"Have a good day Mr. Muzny I look very forward to hearing back from you and to meeting you at Pinehurst."

"I'll be in touch."

Texas Zephyr

"Where is he?" Reba's voice showed more anger than concern.

Jean-François shrugged in his usual dismissive manner with Reba. In true French fashion he never thought of her as his boss or even his peer. The French love women but they don't empower them. Jean-François had a double measure of the French gene.

"Screw you Jean-François. I'm thinking he's hiding out at that pocket sized ranch of his in Giddings. As soon as Arnold finishes his 1:30PM air show I'll have him fly me up there since Milton won't answer his phone and has been missing now for three days.

Aren't you even a little concerned?"

"No. He is a big boy and I am not his mother or his girlfriend."

Reba headed for the flight line and met *Birdman* Bowels before he had time to shut down the 65 horsepower engine that allowed the J3 to punch holes in the sky. He flew with the door open which made it easy for her to lean over and tell him what she wanted. Obviously it had something to do with flying as she was carrying a headset with her.

"Arnold, I need you to fly me to the FiveOnFive Ranch in Giddings right now."

"I don't think I should do that Ma'am. Milton is mighty secretive about that place. Heck, I've only be there once."

"I'm not taking a vote Arnold. I'm giving an answer. We're going to the FiveOnFive Ranch and we're going right now!"

"Yes Ma'am." It wasn't any easier for a Texan to deal with a powerful woman than it was a Frenchman.

Reba glared her displeasure at Arnold *'the Birdman'* Bowles as she slid into the front seat of the Cub.

Arnold never bothered much with the part of the airport that others used. He pushed the throttle all the way forward on the ramp and headed straight for the taxiway intersection with runway 16/34. He would cross both and take off heading west, do a right turn out and be on his way.

Slight forward pressure on the stick raised the tail and transferred lateral authority from the tiny tailwheel to the large rudder. Speed built more quickly as the powerline shifted from slightly up to straight forward. Physics does what physics does 24/7! Arnold, like all good aerobatic pilots, lived by what the gauges said, not what the seat of his pants, told him. As the airspeed indicator crossed 35mph he pulled firmly back on the stick and began his 55 mph climb. The tach indicated the full power limit of 2300 rpm. Arnold eased power back to 2250 rpm as he pivoted the stick to the right while continuing to hold it back and added just a touch more right rudder. As the altimeter hit 950 feet he eased the stick and rudder pedals to their neutral position and reduced power to the cruise setting of 2150 rpm. The plane came level at 1,000 feet which is about as high as Arnold cared to fly.

Reba's eyes were fixed on the bobbing wire coming out of the fuel cap before her. It was what passed for a fuel gauge in the ancient Cub. A more foolproof design wasn't possible; one end of the wire went into a cork floating in the gasoline of the Cubs single 12 gallon fuel tank. The other end passed through a hole in the tank's cap. The pilot and passenger could see the amount of air time they had left measured before them, when the 90 degree bend at the top of the wire touched the cap the engine would stop. Half the wire was visible. They had six gallons of blue fuel to get them where they were going and bring them home.

At cruise, the Cub's airspeed indicator would peg at 65mph. It could go a little faster and sometimes did. Arnold flight planned for 5gph and could cut that to 4gph by managing the tach and leaning carefully. The twenty miles they needed to travel to Milton's FiveOnFive Ranch should take about 20 minutes, almost two gallons of fuel.

This time of day the sky above them was filled with lumpy clouds which meant one thing to those flying below them, a very rough ride. Arnold didn't notice, but Reba thought the plane would surely come apart and they would die at any moment. He watched the back of her neck, if it became really pale he knew she would soon barf. So far she was good and they were already at the half way point.

"Hold on Reba, that's the FiveOnFive Ranch straight ahead."

She strained to see what he saw and tried to find Milton's Cherokee on the ground. It wasn't there.

"He's not there Arnold?"

"I wouldn't be too sure."

"Do you see his plane?"

"No but I expect that it's in the hangar."

They were descending more quickly than Reba liked. Just as she thought a scream was in order, the Cubs fat tires kissed the turf and they rolled towards the hangar camouflaged as a pole barn.

Milton stood in the open doorway on the south end of the barn waved and flashed a toothy grin as Arnold shut down and Reba unbuckled. Tears flowed from her eyes as the fears of what might have been were forced to the side by the joy of what was. Milton was alive!

"Where have you been? I've been worried sick about you." Reba spoke through her sobs and didn't try to hide her feelings.

"I've been here visiting my girlfriend."

Her joy turned to anger as his words sunk in. Had he been playing her all of this time? Was there someone else? Death would be too good for Milton Muzny. She visualized the old Apache practice of staking a honey coated offender spread eagle across an ant bed and leaving him for several days with no food or drink. A long, slow, painful death was just what he deserved.

"Your girlfriend?"

"Come on in and say Hi."

Reba decided that she would do exactly that and once inside she could decide which of them to kill first, probably Milton.

"Is she hiding? Tell her to come out and face the music."

"That's her Reba."

Milton pointed at a small red airplane the likes of which she had never seen before.

"Your girlfriend is an airplane?"

"Well yeah. Did you think I'd been two timing you?"

"Maybe."

"Reba, I'm sorry.

Things have been crowding in on me and I needed some head clearing time so I decided to come up here and spend a couple of hours playing with the *Texas Zephyr*. One thing turned into another. How long have I been here anyway?"

"Three days!"

Arnold didn't want to see this fight. He decided to butt in and change the subject. "Bossman, the *Texas Zephyr* is the most unusual airplane I've ever seen."

"Thank you. I wasn't going for run of the mill."

The airplane was fire engine red with the gold FiveOnFive lightning bolt logo emblazoned along its sides. The ultra-plush natural leather interior was easily visible through the bubble canopy. The pilot's seat, with the passenger's seat in tandem just behind, was slightly forward of the large wing. The **Texas Zephyr** was stunning sitting atop its fixed tricycle gear.

"Well Arnold, only the most astute aviation aficionados can discern that it is a highly modified *VariEze*, the groundbreaking aircraft originally designed by Burt Rutan. It's highly unusual two wing design makes it almost perfect. The small forward canard near the nose is trailed by the large delta wing to the rear. The elevator is the canard. If the plane exceeds the proper angle of attack during a climb the canard stalls and drops the nose which prevents the larger wing from stalling.

It is the second aircraft that cannot stall. The first was the Ercoupe. If an airplane cannot stall, it cannot spin. It is a major safety feature. The lack of flaps which translates into flat approaches and a long landing profile is its only design flaw.

The fuselage and wings are constructed from mold-less composites which make for very slick, rivetless surfaces. The 1974 design speed of 196 mph is still very fast for a fixed gear machine. The highly modified **Texas Zephyr** moves the needle to 270 mph at its expanded cruise altitude of 25,000 feet. The cabin pressurization system makes the ride way up there extremely comfortable. Oxygen masks or cannulas aren't required as cabin pressure keeps the occupants at 8,000 feet. Naturally there is an emergency oxygen system.

The controls have been changed to 100% fly-by-*wireless*. As far as I know, this is the world's first *wireless* aircraft. The advantages are numerous beginning with zero holes penetrating the pressure vessel of the cabin to carry wiring and plumbing to and from the ship's mechanical systems and its flight management computer. The **Texas Zephyr's** cabin has only two holes; one for inletting fresh bleed air from the engine's nacelle and the other for expelling it from the cabin.

The electronics mimic the onboard systems of a *Predator* drone. Off-the-shelf components and systems available to the experimental/homebuilt aviation community have been used extensively to keep costs low. Just as the *Predator*, the **Texas Zephyr** can be preprogramed to fly to any destination in the world with no pilot intervention required, including takeoff and landing.

Arnold notice those three buttons on the panel; red, orange and yellow.

Press the red one and a large parachute is deployed to gently carry the entire aircraft back to earth after it first shuts the motor down, sets the transponder to 7700, activates the ELB and sends out a SPOT message.

The yellow button instructs the airplane to recover from an upset and return to straight and level flight without pilot intervention.

The orange button is the best of all. The Zephyr's motor will not activate until a flight plan is entered into its avionics system, a destination MUST be included. This is an absolute requirement even for VFR flights. When the plane's autopilot is activated, the orange button will blink every fifteen minutes. The pilot then has one minute to press it. If he fails to do so it will sound an alert buzzer for thirty seconds. If he still fails to press the button, the aircraft will assume that the pilot has been incapacitated and will take control of the flight. It will squawk 7700, send out a SPOT message, make a voice transmission to air traffic control on the proper frequency to let them know the status of the flight and that the aircraft intends to proceed to its original destination and land if it is within a 30 minute flight. If that is not the case it will determine the closest airport, proceed to it and land after first alerting air traffic control of its new destination.

If any of that happened, the FAA would have a cow but the pilot and passenger would survive. The plane's priority is crew safety."

"Milton, that's a pretty amazing autopilot. Is it possible for the plane to fly a complete mission without a pilot onboard?"

"No. The autopilot cannot be programmed until the canopy is closed and it deactivates the moment the canopy is re-opened."

"Tell me more about the power system. I get it that it's an electric motor but how can you store enough energy to make a flight of a meaningful duration? Aren't batteries a problem?"

"A Siemens AG motor weighing just 30 pounds and producing 85kW is the heart of its remarkable propulsion system. A Continental 0200 by comparison turns out just 73.5kWs (*about 100 horsepower at full throttle at sea level*) and weighs 170 pounds. Unlike piston engines, electric motors are totally unaffected by altitude, that's the magic that caused me to go with one. Think about that Arnold, it produces as much power at 25,000 feet as it does at sea level. Once it's in the thin air this thing really moves. Piston engines by contrast, even turbo powered ones, produce only 65% or so of their maximum rated power at 25,000 feet.

You're right about batteries. They're no ready for primetime unless you are willing to accept the limitation they place on endurance and range. Even so, you are left with the almost insurmountable issue of recharging time at your destination. Twelve hours for a 'fuel stop' is not acceptable.

The *Zephyr* is a hybrid just like our nation's very first aircraft carrier the Langley was in 1919. Inside the rear cowling where the 0200 used to sit is a small gasoline engine which previously powered a motorcycle. It spins a generator to provide power for the motor that sits in the ducted fan nacelle atop the fuselage.

The BMW i3 works in a similar fashion. In its case, when the car's battery runs low on energy the gasoline powered generator provides the power the drive motor requires. The Chevy Volt is very similar as are all locomotives except they have no batteries at all merely a diesel powered generator that produces power for the trains' electric drive motors.

The *Texas Zephyr* uses the gasoline generator to provide power during takeoff and climb. Once established at cruise altitude, the gasoline engine shuts down and power is drawn from the batteries which are good for two hours when fully charged or from its solar cells. The batteries are hung in a detachable module under the fuselage and can be replaced by a fresh unit in less than 5 minutes.

You may have noticed that the top of the wings are covered with solar cells. Their job is to recharge and augment the battery pack. Above the clouds at 25,000 feet on a sunny day they provide 100% of the power the ship requires. They can easily double its range. I fully expect that on some flights the batteries won't be used at all.

During the descent phase, the motor becomes a generator as it is spun by its windmilling propeller blades. It is capable of replenishing as much as twenty percent of the batteries power on the way down and makes up for the lack of flaps on final approach allowing the *Texas Zephyr* to operate out of strips of just 1,400 feet in length.

At this point everything I've told you that it will do is really what I hope it will do. It has yet to be tested. That starts next week."

"Have you lined up a test pilot?" Reba's voice was filled by the hope for the answer she wanted not the one she felt certain she would get.

"Yes, I have."

"Who?"

"Me, of course, it's my plane and there's no way I'm going to turn over the fun part to someone else.

All of the primary testing was done at Kerrville. The FAA requires the first 25 hours of flight to be completed before the ship can get far away from the field where it was built."

"That makes me feel somewhat better. What testing remains to be done?" Reba quizzed.

"Most of the tricky autopilot features need to be proven, the power management features, cabin pressurization and air conditioning and finally high attitude flight."

"Have there been any problems so far?" Arnold wanted a piece of this project.

"Yes, the nacelle was coming apart at its leading edge. It was made of molded composites. The air friction was just too much for that material. It has been strengthened with that shiny titanium ring you see."

"Did that fix the issue?"

"I think so."

"So what will you do with it?" Reba asked almost mockingly.

"The airplane is all about drawing attention to FiveOnFive and positioning it as a state of the art company. It will be prominently featured in the articles we grant following the US Open. Interviews will only be granted to magazines that agree to include pictures of the airplane as well as the golf clubs. Setting a record or two with this machine will give them all the reason they need to comply."

Pilot Bowles spoke up quickly, "What kind of record do you intend to set?"

"Endurance, speed and distance records are all up for grabs as electric flight is brand new. Setting a speed record for the fastest time from Houston to Dallas in an electric airplane is a piece of cake. The issue will be to pick the city pairs that draw the most attention. Houston to Dallas not so much but Chicago to New York would be a real crowd pleaser as all of the major media providers are headquartered in one of those cities."

"And you have time for all of this?" Reba challenged.

"No, but some lucky pilot boy like Arnold will be pleased to have a shot at all of the fame that comes with being a record maker."

"Milton, if you're asking, I'm in." Arnold couldn't contain his excitement.

"Arnold, I don't know yet who it will be. Keep your nose clean and you'll have a shot."

Milton's phone rang; the screen displayed Guy Smyrle's shinning face. "Hey Guy, what's up?"

"Plenty, you need to get back to La Grange by Saturday afternoon. Earle and a group from the California Attorney General's office have called for a meeting in my office."

"I'll be there. Any idea what's up?"

"Not really. Deidra Longmuffin left a message saying that either Eddie Ray or Leon's ex-wife had been arrested. That's probably not a good thing.

I should know more before the meeting."

"Do you think they plan to arrest me?"

"I think they'd love too but they can't until the charge with Earle is settled."

"Reba, why don't you head back with Arnold? I want to fly the *Texas Zephyr* down. Might be the last chance I get."

"I understand. Stay safe." Reba's tone had switched from combative to supportive.

"Have you heard Milton on the radio, Arnold?"

"No Ma'am, if he took off he's being very quiet. We should be landing in La Grange in about five minutes. You know he could have beaten us back. This plane's awful slow and the one he's flying is really fast."

Practice

Angela knew how to keep the interview on track. "How did you resolve the club issue with the USGA?"

"With a little help from your friends. By the time the Ed Herschel called with the USGA issue every sport's reporter worth his salt had picked up the story. Five unknown golfers all swinging FiveOnFive clubs had qualified for the US Open.

Golf was in the doldrums. The ranks of people playing the game was dwindling to the point that golf courses across the country weren't just hurting they were closing. Tiger Woods had brought interest to the game for a while but it wasn't the kind of interest that caused people to play. It brought them out to watch and tune in but that was it. His type of play actually drove people away as everyone knew they could never play like him so why bother. Fun to watch, impossible to emulate.

Suddenly, the USGA had a positive story that the public would buy into quickly. If these guys can make it to the US Open, golf became the everyman game that Arnold Palmer had caused it to be so many years earlier. Herschel had no interest in killing our clubs; his goal was to endorse them. They could be the secret sauce that brought people back to the game. If it was about the tool and not the guy using it then everyman could play a decent round of golf.

The USGA had reasoned correctly that current golf equipment manufacturers would raise a stink as their sales were already awful and this would make them worse. If FiveOnFive was the answer to every duffer's prayer then the other companys' products would soon be heading to the landfill."

"So what did you do?"

"I jumped in the Cherokee and flew myself and three bags of clubs over to North Carolina. If golf and I were going to say goodbye I wanted it to happen in person so I could plead my case."

Milton filed for KSOP, which is a wonderful airport that serves
Pinehurst and Southern Pines. For a flyin golfer KSOP is as good
as it gets. This time of year the ramp would be covered with
private jets. Some that belonged to players others to golf
equipment manufacturers some to sponsors and dozens to golf
fans.

The 842 nautical mile trip would be made with one fuel stop in
Bessemer, Al. In still air Milton should be there in a little over four
hours. Today the weatherman was calling for a 20 knot tailwind to
shorten his trip to just three hours. The $100 Hamburger website
www.100dollarhamburger.com said there was a restaurant on the
field. He'd be hungry by then and could checkout the competition
while the FBO filled the Cherokee's tanks.

From Bessemer into Pinehurst would take another two and one half
hours assuming the wind was still blowing upstairs.

With a full stomach and a short flight in front of him, Milton filed
VFR. He would fly direct and let the autopilot do most of the work
for him. Autopilots can be a friend or a foe depending on how you
use them. For a sleepy pilot like Milton it could be both at once.
He set the heading to track the GPS course to KSOP and pre-
selected 9,500 feet as his cruise altitude.

On some days, pilot workload at cruise can be nil. This was one of
those days; clear air, sunshine streaming through the windows, a
constant tailwind and no reason to talk to air traffic control or
anyone else. The result can be a nodding pilot. Soon Milton was
sound asleep, speeding along at 180 knots toward Pinehurst. His
route of flight was set to skirt all TFR's, Special Use Airspace and
controlled airspace. He was free to fly without interruption.

Occasionally, we'll read about an airplane that air traffic control
loses contact with. An Air Force fighter is dispatched to check on
it. In the world of golf that's what happened to a flight carrying
legendary player Payne Stewart. His private jet lost cabin pressure
during climb. Tragically neither the pilot nor co-pilot noticed the
problem in time to descend or put on oxygen masks, all aboard
died of asphyxiation. The plane, which was on autopilot, did what

Milton's plane was now doing it flew on. Eventually it ran out of fuel and returned to earth with a pretty good thud, all aboard died. Physics played no favorites that day nor would it today.

"Traffic! Traffic! Traffic!"

The Cherokee's Mode S transponder was connected to both of its Garmin 430's, together they formed a Traffic Information System. The location, direction, altitude and climb/descent trends of every transponder equipped aircraft within 5 miles horizontally and 1200 feet vertically were displayed. Milton had set his unit to sound an auditory alarm if a threat came within two miles horizontally and 500 feet vertically of his Cherokee.

One had.

"Traffic! Traffic! Traffic!"

Startled from his slumber, Milton went into immediate action. The screen was showing traffic in all directions with one threat closing in quickly. He reasoned that it was descending so he disengaged the autopilot with the thumb switch on his yoke and pulled up briskly while adding power. At 11,500 feet a feeling of safety returned to his cockpit. Now it was time to figure out where he was and what was happening.

He had overflown KSOP by about 10 miles and was surrounded by a flock of corporate jets on approach. Milton contacted Charlotte and filed a 'pop up' IFR flight plan back to KSOP.

ATC sequenced him in with the arriving jet traffic. Most were using the ILS approach to runway 5 so he went along with the crowd. When ILS is available most pilots go with it. At more remote airports that have only a GPS approach, they use that.

Milton taxied to a tiedown as directed and placed his fuel order with the lineman. The airport was packed and his spot was far from the terminal so he gladly accepted a ride on the waiting golf car.

Standing just inside the FBO's door was a man who had been watching Milton closely since his landing.

He took a chance and stuck out his hand, "Hi Ed, I'm Milton Muzny. Here's my paperwork and these are my clubs."

His guess was correct.

"Thanks so much Mr. Muzny we look forward to working with you on a quick certification."

"Great. Give me a call when you need me. In the meantime, I think I'll head out to the course. I'd like to see how my boys are doing. Are you headed that way?"

"No, Mr. Muzny not just now. I have some important work to do with your clubs. I'll be up later. We can talk then."

The two men parted company. Milton jumped the shuttle for the course and Ed boarded the USGA jet headed back to their headquarters in New Jersey.

As the shuttle rolled Milton mashed the buttons for the house he had rented for his players. The phone rang but wasn't answered. It was Friday afternoon. His guys were supposed to be on the course and the putting green getting ready for the tournament which would start next week. Alan Levitt, John Murphy, Howard Simms, Steve Samuels and Chuck Bianchi were each committed to winning the US Open.

Milton found them on the practice green.

"Hey guys. How are we doing?"

Steve spoke for the group. "Boss when did you get into town?"

"Just got here and I'll be pulling out first thing in the morning. Let's get back to the house I'd like a briefing."

"Yes sir. I'll get the van." Chuck spoke as hurriedly as he moved.

The veranda of the house overlooked the green of number four. It is one of the featured holes of the tournament. Milton could feel the men's dreams as they looked out at it. They were each frozen with hope.

"Alright then, who'll start?"

Milton wasn't surprised that Howard Simms began. He was the de facto captain of the team. "Mr. Muzny, the first day or two we were here things were hard. The course was tougher in person than the study material made it out to be. The greens are a good deal slower than any of us imagined."

John chimed in "That's all true but now we have it dialed in. Every inch of every fairway and every blade of grass on every green is known to us. We are ready to start playing practice rounds."

"Well then get 'er done boys get 'er done. I'm going to bed."

Chuck showed him to the room that had been set aside for Milton and Reba. Little did these men know or even suspect that Reba and Milton did not share a bed only a growing love that would one day lead them in that direction. That day would arrive when Milton showed up with a ring and a proposal but not until.

Milton rose early and joined the team on the tee. They formed into three twosomes. He moved from cart to cart until he had played a couple of holes with each player.

They were good but he knew that before he arrived. Now they were better. Each had mastered his clubs and the game that he taught that went along with them. As the morning turned into afternoon he was pleased to record pars. All pars, no birdies, no bogies and no eagles. Every fairway was made by every player every time and every green was two putted. More importantly every swing was exactly the same by every man regardless of the club they were swinging. They had each mastered 'Big Hole' putting and the **Five On Five In** strategy.

"Did you think they could hold that through the Thursday and Friday rounds?" Angela was now moving in closer on her prey. Was it strategy and coaching or happenstance?

"Frankly I didn't. I knew that the crowd would cause butterflies and the pairings would cause some missteps. However, I also knew that they didn't need to shoot par on Thursday and Friday to make the cut and avoid being on the bad side of 'Moving Day'. In 2011, Brad Benjamin made the cut with a three over par matching Jason Preeo's 2010 performance. My guys could drop a stroke or two and still be there for Saturday and Sunday."

"But could they win?"

"Absolutely! Graeme McDowell was the US Open Champion in 2010 shooting even par for the four rounds. Phil Mickelson found that even par was good enough for second place in 2002. My guys will be in contention with par. The question is where on the leaderboard even par would be. In some years it's good enough to win. Sometimes par defines middle of the pack."

"In the wee hours of the morning what did you think would happen?"

"I planned on three of our guys getting past 'Moving Day' and one of our guys being in the top ten. That would have made me very happy."

"When did you learn that the USGA was accepting your clubs?"

"It was Wednesday morning. Just before the final pairings were announced my phone rang. It was Ed."

"Mr. Muzny, I have some very good news for you and I believe for the world of golf. Your remarkable clubs are in. By the way, I played a round with them. They are remarkable. First I watched your YouTube videos and then played a round. Mr. Muzny I would really like to own a set."

"WOW! Ed you've made my day and I'll have a set on its way to you this afternoon. It is my gift."

"I can't accept them as a gift Mr. Muzny. If I am to have a set I must pay for them."

"I'll bring your clubs over with me. We can settle up then. I'll be back 'Moving Day'; superstition prevents me from coming earlier."

"Terrific! I'll see you then. Good luck to you and your team."

"When did you get the next call?"

"You mean the one about the lawsuit being filed by every other golf club manufacturer against me and the USGA?"

"Yup, that's the one, who called and what did they say?"

"It was Ed Herschel. He was mortified to give me the news. The litigants were seeking an emergency injunction to keep my guys out of the tournament until the matter was decided. They filed the suit in North Carolina hoping for a good outcome before what they believed to be a favorable judge. They had done more than a little bit of court shopping. I couldn't blame them for that. When you can choose where to file you should always go with the most favorable jurisdiction."

"But the judge didn't give them the injunction did he?"

"Yes and no. He didn't go along with granting emergency relief and keeping my guys out of the tournament. He decided that they could play and he would render his final decision on the facts of the matter before the end of the tournament. So he left us all in the lurch for a couple of days."

"Was it hard to deal with the suspense of it?"

"No not at all. My victory was being in the tournament and getting all of the publicity for FiveOnFive as a result. Orders were coming in so fast that our website crashed. We were selling the sets for $1,000 a piece, bag included. Heck I slept like a baby. I stayed busy making certain that every media outlet got the news release on our story. We used the same techniques that worked with the **Chickenfried Café**. It included shooting, editing and distributing ready to go video pieces for all of our nation's overworked news directors. We positioned ourselves as the underdogs in a true David versus multiple Goliaths story. That was day one's video. Day two featured several weekend golfers who tested our clubs and reported the most amazing round of golf they had ever played. Then we sent promotion sets to the Sport's anchors of the Golf Channel, ESPN, CBS, ABC and NBC.

The story worked for everybody except my adversaries. They looked like bullies who were trying to feather their nest with a product that was no longer competitive.

I knew that someday soon the legal challenge would go away, the US Open would finish and my free publicity engine would sputter to a halt. In the meantime, we were making millions of dollars and thousands of friends."

"What was the basis of the lawsuit?"

"The legacy manufacturers contended that our clubs did not conform and should not be allowed on any golf course let alone the US Open. It was an economic issue for us but a moral issue for the USGA and the PGA. They, the governing body of golf, had approved our club and were now accused of doing so illegally in defiance of their own rules."

"But if you, the USGA and the PGA lost wouldn't your financial exposure have been enormous?"

"Yes, it could have been if you buy the premise that a loss in court would lead to all of our happy customers immediately returning their clubs and demanding a full refund. I never accepted that as a possibility. My thinking was and is that if our clubs improve your enjoyment of the game of golf that you will keep the clubs. It led me to believe that we had a ton of unnamed allies; the golf course operators, be they private country clubs or municipal courses. If peoples' interest in the game was renewed because they once again found pleasure in a round of golf, the businesses that benefitted would become our allies."

"Did you pursue them?"

"Yes, BIG TIME! We mailed, emailed and phoned them. Some made *amicus curiae* 'friend of the court' filings with the North Carolina court that had our case. If the judge was going to consider the financial loss of the legacy manufacturers I wanted him to also consider the financial gain of other industry participants."

"Your players must have been affected by all of this. After all they were being labeled cheaters by association?"

"If they thought that and maybe they did, none of them ever mentioned it to me."

"Milton, what about the '*Friday Afternoon Massacre*'?"

"You label it correctly for that's what it felt like. First my phone rang to let me know it was time to get on over to Pinehurst. All five of our players had made the cut. We'd survived '*Moving Day*'. Then Ed Herschel called to say the judge had issued his opinion. He had granted injunctive relief to the legacy manufacturers. Our guys would not be allowed to play in any PGA or USGA event using our clubs until the matter was resolved. That meant that even though we had made the cut, we wouldn't be allowed to play. I scheduled a Press Conference to take place later that evening at our rental pad in Pinehurst and called NetJets to get me there.

Things were moving very, very quickly. Reba decided to come along. Jean-François packed chickenfried steak dinners for the entire Press Corps onto the plane and came along to supervise serving them. Our golfers would be there to pass them out. We were going for a publicity coup, for FiveOnFive and the **Chickenfried Café**. The best lemonade is made during the worst conditions using the sourest lemons.

Angela, I was about as angry as I have ever been but I decided not to show it. If your opponent hits you hard, he hurts you once. If you let him know you felt it, he hurts you twice. Having a shot at the US Open title was very important to me and my investors not to mention my players. These guys had worked hard, played fairly and deserved their fifteen minutes of fame."

"Milton, I'll bet you knew that many reporters would show up for your quickly announced press conference but did you figure on live, worldwide coverage?"

"No I did not. Cameras were rolling as we setup and didn't stop until we turned out the lights."

"Did you know in advance that Ed Herschel was coming?"

"No that was a complete shock."

"It went down like this:

Ladies and gentlemen thank you very much for coming and I hope you brought an appetite. We've flown in dinner for you from my favorite restaurant, the **Chickenfried Café** of La Grange, Texas. The head chef Jean-François Fournier came alone to supervise. Five of the best golfers in the world will be serving you. One of them may well be the next Champion of the US Open and all of them have earned the right to play. They qualified for that chance on the golf course not in the courthouse. That's the way I think it should be done don't you?

The issue brought before the court addresses the compliance of our clubs with USGA Rule #4. My view is that they are. The USGA and the PGA agree. Only my competitors disagree. Hmmm, I wonder, do you suppose they could have a self-serving motive?

I leave you with this though and then I'll take your questions. The legacy manufacturers changed their design of 'woods' from persimmon to metal years ago. There was no court challenge. Nor did any manufacturer challenge the long shaft putters that some players jam into their chest for stability.

Questions?"

"Mr. Muzny, Sam Donaldson with *Golf Digest*, if you are in compliance, why are you being challenged?"

"Great question. First let's be clear, I am not being challenged. The USGA and PGA are. It is their rule book and their tournament and their authority over the game of golf that is being challenged. I'm comfortable with that. The question you pose should be asked of the legacy manufacturers. Why are they challenging the USGA and the PGA, this great tournament and the game of golf? Why indeed?"

"Mr. Muzny, Amy Ropak, ABC NEWS. You're the only manufacturer that can lay claim to getting all of its players into the final two days of the US Open. How?"

"To begin with they are great and highly disciplined players who worked with us to shift their focus from hitting the 'long' ball to hitting the 'accurate' ball. FiveOnFive equipment is designed for accuracy and consistency not distance. The marriage of great players with great equipment is yielding great results – simple as that."

"I have one follow up question."

"Shoot."

"It has been rumored that at least two and perhaps three of your players may leave the FiveOnFive stable and swing someone else's clubs over the weekend. What can you tell us about that?"

"Amy, that's the first I've heard of it. Heck, they're all in the room. Let's ask 'em.

So are any of you guys jumping ship or are you 'going to dance with who brung you' as we say in Texas? Don't be shy boys if you're staying hold up your right hand."

Two hands went up, Alan Levitt and Howard Simms.

Milton's complexion went ashen. You would have sworn that he had seen a ghost. His head sank for a moment then his fist and his teeth simultaneous clenched.

"Alan and Howard, I appreciate your honor, your loyalty and your friendship. Thank you for standing with me, FiveOnFive and the game of golf.

Guards escort those other three off the premises right now.

Amy it looks like you got a scoop. Congratulations."

Milton smiled. He didn't know why exactly other than it felt good to know who his friends were.

Just then Ed Herschel came through the door with a huge grin on his face. Though he was a modest man he pushed his way onto the stage and stood beside Milton.

No one spoke which was unusual for a room full of reporters. They all knew Ed Herschel and they all wondered why he was here, why he was so happy and what he had to say.

He began to speak, "Milton, members of the press, I have some breaking news.

It has been a busy afternoon.

The USGA and the PGA have been very displeased with the legal challenge brought by a few manufacturers. We would have preferred to work out our differences within the family. Realizing that the judge's ruling might go against us we prepared an emergency appellant strategy. The issue is simple for us. There will be time later for the courts to decide who runs our tournaments, us or the golf club manufacturers. Our confidence in the answer to that question is very high. The problem we were handed this afternoon is one of a very different nature. The legacy manufacturers were using the courts to manipulate the outcome of our tournament by disallowing five players from competing even though they have qualified to do so.

We took the matter to the Supreme Court of the State of North Carolina since the matter was filed in North Carolina. Judge Harriet Williams, just moments ago, vacated the lower court's ruling. FiveOnFive players will be allowed to play."

"John Blackstone, NBC News, Mr. Herschel three of the FiveOnFive players just announced that they are joining up with another manufacturer and will play tomorrow using that manufacturer's clubs. Are you aware of that development?"

"We were approached by the other manufacturer earlier this evening on that subject. I will tell you what I told them,

'No way!'

If those golfers don't play for FiveOnFive we must treat them as a withdrawal simple as that. Milton, help me out here. What is going on?"

"Well Ed this is a tough one. The US Open is an individual not a team competition. I have dismissed three players from my staff for good cause. However, I don't think they intended to withdraw from the tournament nor do I think they should. You are perfectly correct that they must carry the same clubs throughout the tournament and can only substitute in the case of damage. That's the rule. I will sell them each the set of clubs they have been playing with so they can continue. If that works for you Ed, and the players involved I think we're good."

"Great Milton! I hope to see you at the Championship ceremony."

"That'd be great. Now let's eat. I've brought dinner all the way from La Grange, and its gettin' cold."

Angela asked timidly, "I know they played and I know they swung FiveOnFive clubs, how much did you charge them?"

"Nothing."

"Nothing?"

"That's right nothing. Look I was angry and disgusted that they'd thrown me under the bus but I understood and couldn't honestly say that I wouldn't have done the same if I was in their predicament. I thought about charging them $100,000 since that was the amount I had just given them for qualifying.

Instead I brought all five golfers into the living room of the house. Just the six of us and Reba. It was mighty quiet when I began.

First I gave a duffle bag with $100,000 in it to Alan and another one to Howard. That was their due for getting passed *'Moving May'*. It was also the deal I had made with the other three but they had jumped ship so our deal was off or was it?

I brought them forward as a group and asked them a simple question.

'Gentlemen, do you want to compete for the championship of the US Open?'

They each responded with a sheepish head nod.

I then told them, 'look guys, things happen in families. Feelings get hurt and people do things they wish they hadn't. I then handed each man a duffle bag with $100.000 in it.'

We're through here. Now, everybody get to bed, you've got a golf tournament to win and I've got to get back to La Grange.'"

Angela asked the question that was on many minds, "Why did you go back to La Grange? Wouldn't you have preferred to remain at the tournament?"

"I would have much rather remained at the tournament for reasons other than golf. I was scheduled to meet with California law enforcement officials, my attorney and the District Attorney on Saturday afternoon. The US Open played second fiddle to the possibility that I could go to prison."

Weekend

"Mostly I wish for Friday night. Sometimes I pray for Monday morning." Milton reflected.

The wheels of the NetJets Embraer 300 screeched on the pavement of La Grange's runway very early Saturday morning. Guy Smyrle was waiting in my apartment above the **Chickenfried Café**.

"Hey Guy. What brings you out my way this late or should I say this early?"

"Milton I haven't been to bed yet, couldn't sleep. There's a lot happening."

"What's up?"

"Deidra Longmuffin says she found Leon's wife and is with her now. Mrs. Greenfeldt says Leon was alive when he left the hospital with Eddie Ray. She says he walked out at 11:00PM Wednesday.

Two hours later he was in a pine box in the back of Eddie Ray's pickup truck in your driveway.

Milton it's an hour drive from L.A. down to your place so if Mrs. Greenfeldt's story is true Leon was capped pretty quickly after he left the hospital and it had to be pre-planned given the pine box and the travel time."

"Yeah that sounds right."

"Well, none of this looks good for you or Pastor Dave as it blows every word of your story."

"No it doesn't. What it proves is simply that we were misled. I believed a friend who asked for my help. What Eddie Ray told me seemed reasonable, same thing for Pastor Dave."

"I got you Milton, but look at it from the prosecutor's side. You show up with a murder victim, bury him in a pasture and have two hundred large in cash from the victim's safe in your possession."

"The cash came from Leon's safe?"

"That's right.

Turns out that he and Eddie Ray were involved in multiple extortion schemes according to his wife. Eddie Ray would get the money from the victim, take it to Leon, who placed it into a safe in his office until he could get it into Mexico, launder it and bring it back prior to a split with Eddie Ray."

"How did he get it into Mexico?"

"That has nothing to do with you. Why do you care?"

"Look this is all about my life so I want to know every detail. How did he get the cash into Mexico and how did he bring it back?"

"Leon was an offshore fisherman. He would load the cash unto his boat and head out to sea. Somewhere off Baja he'd hook a big fish and stuff the cash inside. He'd then head into port, make pictures with his trophy fish on the dock, wait until dark, remove the cash and have the fish butchered and the meat given to the poor. The people loved him. The cash would be deposited into a Mexican bank and wired to a shell company's account in the Caymans. From time to time he'd bill that company for legal services, as he was a lawyer. A payment would be wired to his office account in California; done deal, clean money."

"So why did he and Eddie Ray have a falling out. She told Deidra Longmuffin that Leon got greedy and kept a longer end of the take than he gave to Eddie Ray."

"How does she know all of this?"

"How does she know that her husband was in the extortion business?"

"Yeah and how did she know he was shorting Eddie Ray?'

"She was part of the extortion scheme."

"Really?"

"Yeah.

Leon was in his early sixties. His wife is twenty-three and semi-gorgeous. Together they would target an older highly successful married dude. Typically one who kept his boat at the marina in Redondo where Leon had his boat or at their country club.

Candace, that's her name, would bump into the mark, form a friendship etc. etc. etc. Then Eddie Ray would show up in the guy's office or at his home playing the role of her angry brother. He'd be armed with pictures, a video or two and a threat. Pay up and leave my sister alone or I'll take all of this to your wife and kids.

It's a stupid plan that worked over and over again."

"Do you believe her story?"

"Parts of it make sense."

"Well it's all very interesting. Do you think Eddie Ray killed the guy?"

"I don't know nor do I care.

The meeting is going to take place here at 8AM."

"Here?'

"That's right at 8AM which is just five hours from now. Are you prepared?"

"I think so. What do you expect will happen?"

"You'll to be taken into custody?"

"Dave?"

"He'll be in attendance and they'll have a set of cuffs his size as well."

"So then what happens?"

"I'll see what the charges are and what evidence they have and then we'll begin to fight back."

"What happened to District Attorney Earle, I thought his charges here in Texas would keep me out of jail in California."

"It will but it won't keep you from being charged. Look, Milton I know it's scary and I'm not even gonna' tell you that I know how you feel because I don't. What I can tell you is that whatever happens tomorrow helps us. We need to know what they've got before we can defend against it. At the end of the day what we have trumps whatever they have but law is a lot like playing bridge. It matters how you play your cards sometimes more than which cards you have."

"I'll bite. What do we have that's so powerful?"

"Innocence, you and Pastor Dave are innocent."

"You're right about that but I suspect we wouldn't be the first innocent men to be sent to prison."

"Milton, I'll be back here at 7:30AM. Try to get some shut eye."

The State of California's Grumman 550 was heading at high speed towards La Grange, Texas. The state's Attorney General had come aboard at the last minute. This was an election year and this case was in the news. She would handle it personally.

"Madam Attorney General forgive me for waking you but Major Garrison of the State Highway patrol is on the radio and needs to talk to you."

"No problem. Can I take it back here?"

"Yes Ma'am. Just push that button when you're ready."

"Major Garrison, what's up?"

"Madam Attorney General we have located Eddie Ray Farrell's car and are presently involved in a high speed pursuit of it. The suspect is believed to be its sole occupant."

"Where?"

"Interstate 5 between San Clemente and Oceanside."

"Isn't that stretch all within the Marine Corps Base Camp Pendleton?"

"It is."

"So he has no opportunity to exit until he gets to Oceanside?"

"That's right. We've shut down the freeway on both sides just north of Oceanside and setup a blockade on the southbound side to greet him."

"How long?"

"It will go down in the next ten minutes. One other thing you should know. There has been gunfire and one of our officers is being transported to the hospital. He may not survive."

"I see. Keep the media off his family until I get back."

"Will do."

Like many Californians, Eddie Ray was a car nut. His ride was a perfectly restored 1960 Lincoln Continental convertible triple black. It was a beautiful machine with a stock 430 cubic inch engine which Eddie Ray had blueprinted and balanced during the restoration process. It rolled. On this night, it was having no problem pacing the California Highway Patrol at 130 mph plus as they passed the San Onofre Nuclear Generation Station.

The windshield of the road humping Lincoln suddenly lit up like a nuclear explosion as the CHP manning the roadblock switched on their portable stadium lights. Thirty officers crouched behind a barricade of highway cruisers let loose with a salvo of M16 fire. Every third round they fired was a tracer which made it easy to target Eddie Ray's battered battlewagon. Almost as quickly as it came into view it swerved and just as suddenly rolled. Given its speed and the violence of the hail of gunfire that reached out to greet it, the Lincoln was reduced to a storm of flying parts.

"Cease fire. Cease fire."

The order was given and obeyed. Silence returned to this part of the California coast. Cautiously a helmeted, flak jacketed SWAT team moved out towards the part of the wreckage that contained the front seat and it's mangled beyond recognition occupant. Clearly he was dead.

"Stand down. Let's get this mess cleaned up. Load the body unto the chopper. The sooner we get it to the crime lab the sooner we can get a positive ID and close the case of Eddie Ray Farrell."

The Grumman 550 touched down in La Grange rolled to a stop and taxied to a parking spot. The stairs came down almost at once. The door popped open and the passengers led by Attorney General Charlotte Hamilton scrambled to the tarmac.

District Attorney Earle was there to meet them. As they approached the airplane watching deck of the **Chickenfried Café** Guy Smyrle waved from a table where he sat enjoying a plate of Beignets and a pot Chicory coffee.

"Join me please, these are the best Beignets in the history of earth and this Chicory coffee will wake you up and put hair on your chest. I can guarantee you that?"

"Thanks for the warning on the coffee. I think I'll do well to avoid the result you mention." Attorney General Hamilton laughed as she spoke.

Everyone was seated as two male servers brought plates of beignets, pitchers of iced water, milk, chocolate milk and two pots of coffee; one with chicory the other without.

Unexpectedly, the servers pulled up chairs and seated themselves with the rest of the group. Jaws dropped.

Guy smiled broadly as he gestured and introduced, "Milton Muzny and Pastor David Holman."

District Attorney Earle was in on the joke and couldn't hold back his laughter as color returned to the checks of their California guests.

"It is always good to begin a matter as serious as this with an air of cordiality." Charlotte Hamilton signaled that it was time to begin.

"I agree." Guy wanted her to get used to the sound of his voice.

"Mr. Smyrle I assume you represent both Mr. Muzny and Reverend Holman?"

"That's correct."

"Do you wave reading them their rights and will you allow us to question your clients?"

"No!"

"No?"

"No, first we'd like to know why you're here and what you intend?"

"My apologies I had assumed that District Attorney Earle had informed you."

"It'd be best if you assumed nothing from this point forward and that you agree to the presence of our stenographer Ms. Graybar."

"Agreed, as to the stenographer. As to our purpose, we are here to formally charge your clients with second degree murder and to ask that Mr. Earle agree to allow our case to precede his as ours is more serious. Finally, we seek immediate extradition of your clients to our custody."

"My, my you do have high hopes and a full agenda. We move a little more deliberately in Texas. Let's start with a formal presentation of the charging document accompanied by all of the evidence you have to support those charges."

"Certainly, Mr. Smyrle. This folder contains everything we have presently as well as the formal charge."

"Thank you Ma'am. Please continue to enjoy breakfast. My clients and I will now take your leave. I'll be back to you as soon as I have had a chance to review your filing and your evidence."

"Not so fast Mr. Smyrle. The State of California demands a response as to our standing and extradition request from Mr. Earle."

Ronnie Earle stammered a bit as he replied, "Guy, I'm afraid I have some bad news for you. I have decided to drop all of my charges and to place your clients under arrest subject to the charges formally brought by the State of California."

"How courageous of you Ronnie! Frankly, I expected a bit better of an official sworn to uphold the rights of the citizens of Fayette County, Texas.

Milton, Dave there is nothing we can do about the arrest. Let's agree to go peaceably to the County jail. I have Judge Belmont standing by as I suspected this might happen. He will set bail on this matter and schedule an extradition hearing based on the courts calendar."

"Come on Mr. Smyrle. Don't make this harder than it has to be." Charlotte was angry. She wasn't used to not getting her way.

"Ms. Hamilton we have a quaint practice of following the law in this state. People get charged, then there is discovery, then there is a trial. If they are convicted and only then do we incarcerate them. We place a high value on the rights of our citizens and place those rights above the desires for expediency of an official of a sister state. Ronnie, if it would be all the same to you we'll surrender at the courthouse. Grant us at least that courtesy."

"Sorry Guy.

Deputy, cuff Mr. Muzny and Pastor Holman, take them into custody and transport them to the cop shop. I'll meet you in the booking room.

Guy, I guess I'll see you after a while."

"Ronnie are you sure you wanta' behave this way? La Grange is a small town. Milton and Pastor Holman are important members of the community. You're gonna' alienate a lot of people."

"Guy, I see it differently. Justice wears a blindfold when it comes to people's status. If I don't treat the highest and mightiest among us in the same manner as the lowest then I have failed as a public servant, a citizen and a man."

"That's horseshit Ronnie. It may sound good in some grade 'B' movie but it doesn't wash well in the real world."

"Ronnie, Guy just stop arguing and let's get this done. I've got a lunch meeting at the church. The cuffs won't bother me or Milton and we've never ridden in the back of a police car. It may be fun."

Pastor Holman spoke as a man who served the Lord above, rather than any man below.

California radio and TV was covered with reports of Eddie Ray's fate. Everyone felt safer knowing that this common criminal had meant his just reward and the state had been spared the expense of a trial. That is everyone except Eddie Ray Farrell who still walked among us.

Backed into a prime spot at the Delmar Beach parking lot, Eddie Ray sat in the living room of his ancient Bounder motor home, ate breakfast and watched TV. He was shocked by the reports of his untimely death and the joy it seemed to bring to so many. The man on the street interviews that accompanied the report were chilling.

Before long the police would know that he wasn't dead and who was. Then his problems would multiply. He now knew that he could be shot by the overzealous actions of a police department anxious to apprehend him.

Two hours later, the news came. The deceased was Hudson James Camerman, a wealthy California land developer.

Eddie Ray hit the Favorites button on his phone and mashed the one next to the picture of Candace Greenfeldt.

Candy's phone rang. Both she and Deidra watched the picture of Eddie Ray fill the screen.

"Answer it!" Deidra demanded.

"Hey stranger."

"I'm going in, you should too."

"Together?"

"No."

"Where are you?"

"San Francisco."

"How 'bout you?"

"Santa Barbara."

The lies they both just told were actually a preplanned coded message they used during their grifts. San Francisco meant 'are you alone', Santa Barbara answered 'no I'm not'.

"OK then. Good luck. Lawyer up."

Lawyer up was code for say nothing until your lawyer gets there. They both used Guy Smyrle's brother Larry. He had moved to LA many years ago and quickly gained a reputation as the go to guy for big problems. What they had qualified.

Eddie Ray hung up and mashed Larry Smyrle's smiling face.

"Larry, I'm ready to come in."

"Fine, I'll meet you in Santa Monica. When can you be there?"

"It's a three hour drive from where I am."

"I'll see you there at 9AM. Say nothing and do nothing until I get there. What are you driving?"

"An old Bounder motorhome."

"Cool park in front in the no parking zone. That'll be fun."

"I'm on the way."

Larry's phone rang again.

"Larry, its Candace. I'm coming in."

"Let's do it at Santa Monica. Can you be there at 9:30AM?"

"Yes."

"Make it so."

Soon Eddie Ray and Larry Smyrle found themselves sitting across from each other in a conference room in the Santa Monica police station.

"Eddie Ray it's time to lay it all out for me. This lady is a court reporter she'll be recording every word of the conversation we have in this room. The record she makes can be used in a court of law as part of your defense. You are not waving attorney client privilege in any way by accepting this procedure as I cannot use it or supply it to anyone else without your permission."

"Sure where shall I start?"

"Let's go with a casket.

You show up at Milton Muzny's place two hours after you and Leon left his hospital together with a casket containing Leon Greenfeldt's body.

Please explain."

"The casket was filled with cash not Leon."

"Really?"

"Yup!

I dropped Leon off at his house and headed home. Fifteen minutes later I got a call from Candace to come back and pick up the casket which was merely Leon's latest scheme to move money out of the country. He'd had it with stuffing fish.

My job was to get the casket to Beaumont, Texas and have it buried. Leon would show up later to exhume it and have it shipped to Mexico for burial. At twenty million dollars plus, it was the biggest shipment we had ever attempted.

I took the casket to Milton's place and fed him a line. He bought it hook line and sinker."

"So Milton wasn't knowledgeable of your scheme in anyway?"

"That's correct."

"Well that's an interesting story but several months later the cops dug up the casket and found Leon inside with a hole in his head and none of the cash you've just mentioned. Seems odd wouldn't you say?"

"Well yeah, I'll give you that."

"So how did the cash get out and Leon crawl in?"

"I have no idea."

"OK let's backup a little. Did you ever see the casket opened? Did you see the cash inside it?"

"No to both questions."

"So Leon could have been inside the whole time for all you know?"

"Well that's possible I suppose."

"So you may have been as big a dope as you thought Milton was?"

"Anything is possible."

"You can see why the police would have a problem with your story can't you?"

"I can but I acted on what Candace told me."

"You can imagine the problems with that can't you? Her character is a little south of sterling."

Larry and Eddie Ray parted company. Eddie Ray went back to a holding cell. Larry went to another conference room to meet with Deidra.

"Well Deidra, what have you got for me?"

"A big stack of oddities and not much else I suppose.

Eddie Ray was Candace's hey boy. Like so many others. He fell in love with her and believed she was in love with him.

In a very strange way, she was in love with Leon and did exactly what he told her to do. Maybe he was a father figure. I can't say but she was definitely under his spell."

"Did she shoot him?"

"No I don't think so. It's possible but the story she tells makes sense.

She and Leon helped slide the casket into the bed of Eddie Ray's truck. Then they said goodbye, gave him a big thumbs up and sent him on his way.

Here's where the story takes an interesting turn. There being no honor among thieves, Leon decided to trail Eddie Ray to Milton's house. Candace claims that she never heard from him again. She filed a missing persons report the next day. His car was found two weeks later in an alley behind a school a block away from Milton's house. The school's janitor called to report it. Its discovery started police on the track that led to the Morehead's pasture.

They interviewed Candace multiple times and were never able to shake her story."

"What did she tell them?"

"Well here's the lead detective's report. Her story is simple. My husband came home from the hospital driven here by his friend Eddie Ray Farrell. He felt fine and told her he was going to his office to catch-up on a few things and expected to be back in an hour or so. She has stuck with that story like white on rice."

"Can she explain why her husband felt the need to go to his office near midnight?"

"She was asked about that repeatedly and responded simply that he was a workaholic and the hour was not unusual for him. Several of his associates support her contention."

"So what does your gut tell you?"

"Candace appears to be a very simple woman who has lived a highly compartmentalized life. Truth for her lives differently within each of her life's segments. What is true in one may not be true in another.

Bottom line, she is a survivor."

"We have to accept that there was something heavy inside the pine casket other than Leon as Leon helped Eddie Ray load it unto the truck or we have to believe that Eddie Ray lied and Leon was in the casket. How can we know which is true?"

"Well Leon's car got itself to that alley somehow and his blood is spattered all over it. That says that Leon was murdered in his car and not at his house. So why would either Eddie Ray or Candace or both go to the trouble of capping Leon in his car on a street far from his home and then stuff him into a casket, nail it shut in the middle of the street and truck it to Milton's house. That could have happened but their best opportunity to kill him and place him in the casket was at his home."

"Do we know who made the casket?"

"Yeah, it was a handyman that did work on the Greenfeldt's house. He made ten for Leon the week before he disappeared. Candace told him they were for their Jewish friends. The finished caskets were stacked in the garage. Eight are still there today."

"Eight?

Did you say eight?"

"I did. Why?"

"Well two are missing. Leon was buried in one. Where's the other?"

"Larry I don't know. I missed it. You're right."

Eddie Ray was pacing in his cell as the guard came to escort him back to the interview room.

"Eddie Ray I'm Detective Garradelli this is my partner Detective Phillips. We have a few questions for you."

"Really, where's my lawyer? I have the right to have him present during any questioning don't I?"

"It's up to you whether you answer or not but we have the right to ask. So here goes.

How is it that Hudson James Camerman was in possession of your car last night and why was he running from us? By all accounts, he was an upstanding member of the community and was not under investigation for anything by anyone. Yet he ran.

Why?"

"I think I'll just punch the lawyer button again guys."

"Well that's your right Mr. Farrell. By the way, did you know that we have Mrs. Greenfeldt in custody?"

"No. Has she done something?"

"We think she's an accomplice to her husband's murder. We intend to charge her and you as well. One of you will make a deal and grab a 'get of jail free card' for telling us the story. The other will go away for a very longtime as in forever.

Think about that Mr. Farrell. Now we'll we get your attorney for you.

While you're talking to him, we'll be talking to her.

How old is she?

Twenty-three?

Shouldn't take too long."

"Do what you need to do."

Many miles away a similar scene was being played out in the Fayette County Courthouse.

"Judge, my clients are upstanding citizens with substantial ties to the community. We request that they be released pending trial and we object to the highhanded actions of the Attorney General of the State of California. Trying to extradite before formally charging my clients with a crime is most unusual."

"Yes, yes Mr. Smyrle I sort of figured you felt that way. Now, let me hear from you Madam Attorney General?"

"Good Morning your honor. The State of California has formally charged Mr. Muzny and Reverend Holman with manslaughter; those charges have been lawfully filed in San Diego County, California in accordance with California law. Manslaughter is a serious charge in every state, Texas included. We are requesting that the accused be extradited to California to stand trial and suggest that the subject of bail is a matter for the court of jurisdiction on the manslaughter charge which is San Diego County."

"OK, I get the picture. When is trial scheduled on these charges?"

"The trial date has not been set as our investigation is ongoing."

"So you want to grab a couple of our citizens and move them to California for an indefinite period of time while you complete your investigation? Well, that doesn't work for me.

Let's do it this way.

You give me a shout when you've got final charges and a trial date and I'll consider your motion at that time. Mr. Smyrle I'm prepared to release your clients on their own recognizance if you will agree to make them available for questioning by the representatives of the California Attorney General's office. Those examinations are to take place in Fayette County at reasonable times with reasonable notice.

Now Mr. Earle you release these boys from your custody immediately and do not re-arrest them on any charges related to this matter until we are presented with final formal charges from California accompanied by a trial date.

That said Madam Attorney General there can be no extradition as the parties you seek to extradite are not in custody.

Got it?"

"Yes Judge, I understand your rulings and with respect to you I will appeal."

"Please spend all the time and money you wish in our great state Madam Attorney General. These proceedings are ended.

Milton is your restaurant open? I'm mighty hungry."

"I look forward to serving you Judge."

"I'll be there to ask the Blessing your Honor." Pastor Holman spoke forcefully.

"Well Milton it looks like you and Dave have dodged that bullet for a while." Reba was more thrilled than she sounded.

"Well Baby Girl that's right we have. Can you do me a big favor and get us a NetJets flight to Pinehurst early tomorrow morning. We should be on hand just in case. Reba have them send a Citation X. Let's go in style."

"In case?

Twitter is on fire with the news that three of our boys are among the leaders and the other two are holding their own. I think FiveOnFive is going to win this thing."

"Well if we do, I want you to do the honors of standing with our winning boy as he accepts the cup. I'm too shy and you're too pretty. I want America to get a look at you."

"Milton, you truly are a silver tongued Oreo. Now let's get over to the restaurant we've got a line of folks waiting to get in."

"Guy, what do you make of what's going on in California with the Leon Greenfeldt situation? Hudson James Camerman, whoever he is, was killed last night in Eddie Ray Farrell's car following a high-speed chase down the I-5. Candace Greenfeldt and Eddie Ray have turned themselves in. What's up with all of that?"

"Did you know that my brother Larry is representing both of them?"

"No I didn't know that you had a brother?"

"I do, he's a pretty fair country lawyer as they say."

"Have you spoken with him?"

"Earlier this morning."

"What's his take?"

"He thinks Hudson James Camerman acted alone and mentioned something about an extortion plot. Apparently Hudson James Camerman had been a mark of Leon, Candace and Eddie Ray. Later he turned the tables on them. That's what Larry, my Bro. thinks led to Leon's death."

"Man that is an interesting tale. Let's go get some lunch. If you wanta' invite the Californians I'm OK with it."

"No, I'm good. Plus they've gotta' get over to Austin to file their appeal."

"What are their chances with that?"

"They haven't got a snowball's chance in hell.

Think about it this way. Pastor Dave had nothing to do with any of this? Your story is a little harder to unravel but bringing a manslaughter charge against Dave is just silly. Even so, they have him facing the same charges as you. It's just crazy"

"Good to know.

Guy, all of this sucks. This is my weekend to be with Alan Levitt, John Murphy, Howard Simms, Steve Samuels and Chuck Bianchi over at the US Open. Instead here I am screwing around with all of this crap. Pardon my French but I can't get my head around what's happening to me.

I've got a restaurant business that's going great. We're opening two new joints next week. My golf business is booming to the point that we can't keep up with the orders. The experimental plane that is the test bed for a ton of products and systems I want to sell is just amazing, really amazing. Yet here I am focusing on something that isn't even a small part of my life plan. All I did was help a friend."

"Quit feeling sorry for yourself Milton. Because of that act of kindness you own a highly successful chain of restaurants, you're on your way to winning the US Open, that stupid airplane you play with may turn into something worthwhile and you've reunited with Reba which is probably the most important thing in your life."

"Yeah you're right. Did you get that will drawn up I asked you about?"

"Got it in my briefcase. All it needs is your signature. It's pretty short and sweet as all it does really is give half of everything you own to Reba and the other half to the Global Wildlife Foundation, whatever that is.

By the way, I tried to do some checking on Herbert Anthony Franklin the guy who heads it up and found nothing. I mean nothing. The foundation is registered in the Caymans for whatever that's worth. I also bought the $10,000,000 life insurance policy you wanted."

"Whip it out and loan me your pen. Let's put some ink on that paper."

"You sure?"

"Yeah, I'm sure."

"Ok, its official you're now worth more to Reba dead than alive.

Does she know about this?"

"No. Figured I'd fill her in on the way back from Pinehurst."

"Well let's get moving. I'm hungry."

"Me too. Where's Reba?"

"I think she went to get her car. She's probably waiting at the curb."

There she was and off they went.

"Reba, when are we going?"

"The plane should be here right after lunch."

"How are we doing over there?"

"Alan Levitt, John Murphy and Howard Simms, finished the day at even par which has them in the top 15 on the leaderboard. Steve Samuels and Chuck Bianchi are tied at two under just three strokes behind the leader."

"Baby Girl, we could win this thing."

"I know. The phone's been ringing off the wall. Every reporter in the world wants to talk to you and every golf equipment store and country club wants to sell FiveOnFive clubs. Milton, the **Chickenfried Chicken Coop** took 3,753 orders this morning. That's almost $4,000,000 in sales in half a day!"

"If it's OK with you I'm going to skip lunch and go upstairs and lay down. I'm whipped. You're welcome to join me."

"Does that offer come with a proposal and a ring?"

"It does as soon as we get back."

"So this is a proposal to propose? I think I'll wait for the real deal, ring and all."

"Your loss."

Milton dialed Steve Samuels who answered quickly, "Yes sir boss."

"Hey Stevie, I want you to know that I think of you as the captain of our team and I want you to keep everybody pumped up for tomorrow. I'm coming in with Reba. So what do you think our chances are?"

"Well we've got the course dialed in. Our scores improve every day. Our competitors are all over the place. We've found a line on 4, and 16 that allows us to birdie. It's taken us all this time to find it but two of us now consistently birdie those holes and the other three are committed to follow our path tomorrow. I think we could take five of the top ten spots and perhaps finish first and second. How'd you like that."

"I'd be very pleased if all of you just finished in the top half. Do that and we're home free anything more and we're in high cotton. Now have a quiet evening and don't count your chickens before they hatch. Get to bed early and alone!"

"Yes sir boss."

There aren't many jets that land at La Grange. When Milton heard the thunder of the Citation's huge engines go to full power as the pilot flipped on the thrust reversers he knew it was time to go.

Reba knocked on his door and asked sweetly, "do you want any food put on board?"

"No Baby Girl, I'm too nervous to eat."

Reba knew that already but was very surprised to hear him admit it.

Milton had chosen the Citation X for this trip for a reason other than luxury, though it certainly was that. One of his idols was Arnold Palmer who was the greatest golfer who ever lived and a very good pilot. Arnold's last plane was a Citation X. It was a very comfortable plane for its passengers and was the fastest corporate jet in the skies with the ability to cruise just over 600 mph. Unfortunately NetJets had a strict rule against anyone other than their pilots sitting in the cockpit even if that person was a well-qualified pilot like Milton.

"Reba, lets enjoy this flight shall we?"

"Heck yes.

Can you believe that we're on our way to the US Open golf tournament and that a golfer swinging your clubs might win?"

"I can. My problem is what to do about it. Our order rate is way too high for us to catch up anytime soon. So I've got to find a way to beef up production quickly or sell the company while it's on a roll."

"Sell? I never thought I'd hear you say such a thing."

"Reba, some people are good at running things and some people are good at starting things. I'm the later kind. Every now and then I get an itch that needs to be scratched and then I get bored with it."

"You can't be bored with FiveOnFive already."

"Oh yes I can and I am. What else is there for me to do? From here on out, it's just grinding it out. That's not me.

I want to focus on the ***Texas Zephyr.***"

"What about the **Chickenfried Café**?"

"Oh I'll keep that forever because I like flying airplanes. Can you imagine any other business that allows me to fly to an airport and not have to leave it to do my job? If I could combine it with an airplane manufacturing company life would be super sweet.

Its full speed ahead for the **Chickenfried Café** and time to sell FiveOnFive."

"Who'll buy it?"

"Well I figure we'll be approached by one or more of the incumbent manufacturers."

"Have you thought about price?"

"I'd like your help on that, Reba."

"Well, we've just started and have done no advertising or promotion. Earlier we discussed this morning's orders, about $4,000,000. Using that as a daily average going forward we'd see

$1.4 billion in sales this year, our first year. Can you believe I just used the 'B' word as in billion? Our net profit is 20% so we should net $280,000,000 this year. Five times net would be very fair so $1.2 billion."

"Stock or cash?"

"They'll want to swap stock and put a lock on when we can sell it. I don't like that because it's a lot of money to bet on somebody else's abilities."

"Agreed. So what should we shoot for?"

"I suggest $500,000,000 cash. That's a big discount for them and a whale of a payday for us."

"OK half a billion it is? If not, not."

Reba had ordered a big black limousine to whisk them to the course. The FiveOnFive flags were affixed to the front of the car in Brigadier General fashion. It was impressive. They had changed on the plane. Reba looked like two billion dollars. Milton looked like Milton which was everyone's idea of a riverboat gambler.

The leader board was visible as they passed through the circular driveway in front of the clubhouse. Howard Simms was number three and Chuck Bianchi was on top. Somehow he was four under as he walked off 16.

"How can that be, Milton?"

"Easy, our guys have dialed in the course. They know how to par every hole and have figured out how to birdie 4 and 16. Howard is putting that knowledge into practice better than the others and the whole group if maintaining at least par and sometimes picking up a birdie. It's the clubs and the strategy. Both are working.

Reba, I'm not sure selling makes any sense. We could run this into the biggest thing that's hit golf in over a hundred years. I'm thinking about a magazine and a cable channel all our own. It's feeling too early to get out."

"What about the money?"

"Life isn't about money. It's about time. You can always get more money and with money you can buy health or a facsimile of it. The one thing you can never buy more of no matter how much money you have is time. So all that matters is what you do with the time you've got. Does it make you smile and does it give your life purpose and meaning."

"Why Milton, I never knew you were so philosophical. I get it by the way and I agree and would add that life is also about people. Living as a hermit is no good unless you're sociopathic."

"So it's agreed, we're not selling?"

"Milton, what's all this we business about? Is there a ring and a proposal in my future?"

"Could be, that's what makes Monday's so special. Everybody starts a new chapter on Monday morning. Let's just see what Monday brings."

Alan Levitt flung the door open of the limo and shouted enthusiastically, "Reba, Milton if we hurry you can see Chuck and Howard finish their rounds. Chuck's walking up to the green now and Howard's waiting to tee off."

"OK Baby Girl let's get 'er done."

They sprinted hand in hand like the high school sweethearts they once were.

Chuck was lining up a 40 foot putt for his birdie. He finally eased his putter back to send his ball on its final journey. The ball ran towards the hole and slowly came to a stop three feet to the right of the cup. The distance was perfect, the line was not. Chuck approached the ball, lined up the three footer with the same care he had taken with the forty footer that preceded it. There are no gimmies in golf, every putt is as important as every other putt. Chuck leaned over the ball and prayed as he stroked it, just as he always did. The ball found the cup just as all of his putts inside five feet did. Chuck was tied for third place on the leader board.

"Baby Girl, we may never sell!"

"Shhh! Howard's hitting his approach shot."

The high arching eight iron shot came to rest just twenty feet from the cup. The crowd roared. Reba grabbed Milton. Life was getting better.

As Howard walked onto the green and tipped his hat, the crowd exploded. A hero had been born. Howard Simms an unknown teaching pro from Bella Vista, Arkansas had become a star in just two days.

Howard missed the twenty footer, which was to be expected. No one would have believed it possible for him to fail with the 10 inch putt that remained but he did. Howard had choked under the pressure. His name on the leader board dropped from first to second. Star yes, golf god, not quite yet.

Reba and Milton decided to give the boys some space for now and join them for a little celebration at the house later. There was plenty of time.

As they walked past the sponsor tents towards the club house, their presence attracted the attention of Joe Nellis, the President of the Golf Club Manufacturers Association.

"Reba, Milton wait-up!"

"He knew them by sight. They knew him not at all."

"Can I help you?" Milton inquired of the fast approaching stranger.

"On the contrary, I can help you."

"I didn't know I needed any help."

"Well you do and I'm just the man who can provide it. Let me come straight to the point. I'm Joe Nellis with the Golf Club Manufacturers Association. We've got a great deal to talk about."

"Really? Like what for instance?"

"For starters, I'd like to invite you to join our association."

"Well that's nice and I can guess how that helps you but how exactly does it benefit me?"

"Let's do this. We're having a little get together this evening at my place on the 12th green. Why don't you and your lady stop by? The CEO of every club manufacturer will be there. I know they'd like to meet you."

"I can give you a definite maybe. This is a pretty big day for FiveOnFive. Our schedule is jammed."

"Mr. Muzny I can think of $100 million reasons you might want to drop by."

"Well that is interesting and for $100 million I might show up or I might not for $500 million I could almost guarantee it."

"Shall we say 7:30PM?"

"Reba can we work these boys in?"

"I suppose so sugar."

Milton and Reba arrived at the FiveOnFive house shortly after Howard and Chuck walked through the door and collapsed on the sofa.

"Howard. You're the man. As a matter of fact you're all the man. Your job was to learn this course and to shot par. You've all done that and you're all on the leader board. How in the heck Howard and Chuck got near the top of it is beyond me. Congrats to everybody you each deserve it.

So what about tomorrow and what about winning this thing? Get it out of your minds. We're not here to win. We're here to compete.

We've already won. The FiveOnFive staff will now be a factor in every USGA and PGA tournament from this day forward."

"Milton. It ain't good enough. I wanted to win and I blew it. The pressure got to me." Howard almost cried as he spoke.

"No Howard, that isn't what happened. You forgot for a minute 'to dance with who brung 'ya' and to do focus on your goal. Winning isn't getting a cup and a big check. Winning is about knowing where you have to put the ball with each shot, remembering how to do that and executing your plan. We don't play 'fancy' golf we play 'on purpose' golf. We hit our targets with each stroke. The leader board isn't our goal it is the result of achieving our goals.

Don't forget that tomorrow. Play each stroke and put the hole, the round and the tournament out of your mind."

"Yes sir boss."

"Now Reba and I gotta' go into the camp of our enemy. Wish us luck."

They walked hand in hand to Mr. Nellis' house it wasn't that far away and they enjoyed the time they had apart from everybody else.

"Hi Joe."

"Hi Milton, welcome Reba. Glad you could make it."

A hush fell over the room. Everyone sat down. Clearly there would be no 'get acquainted' chit-chat. These guys were in a rush to get something done.

Joe as the group's representative spoke. "Look Milton, it's no secret that FiveOnFive has disrupted things for our group. We tried to neutralize you in the courts. It appears that isn't going to work and even if it did we're left with the problem that our sales have gone to zero. Joe 'Six Pack' wants your equipment not ours. So we're here, checkbooks open to buy you out. Your clubs will usher in a new day and we want to own tomorrow just as we owned yesterday. You mentioned $500 million. We're prepared to do that."

"Well I am flattered but not interested. You see I've wanted to be in the golf business for many years. Now I am but I am equally interested in bringing the game of golf back to life. We can do that better together than I can alone. You five manufacturers have forgotten more about marketing and manufacturing than I will ever know. I didn't come here tonight to sell out I came here to join up. I want to be part of your association. I want to be a member of the Golf Club Manufacturers Association."

"Milton, it's very, very humbling that you want to join us but your presence will put the other five out of business within a year. You've almost accomplished that in the past week alone."

"Hear me out gentlemen. I want and need your five hundred million and you want and need my clubs. Let's load up everybody's plate.

I'm prepared to issue each of you a license to manufacturer my clubs and to provide you with access to the equipment we use to make it possible. You'll be up and running by the end of next month. I'll continue to build and sell 'em too."

"You want $100 million from each of us for a license to manufacturer your clubs? That's way too much."

"Consider the alternative; bankruptcy. No I'm not offering you a manufacturing license. I'm suggesting a royalty agreement. Anyone who wants to participate can. The $100 million covers the initial two year royalty period and the technology transfer. After two years you'll pay me $5 a stick.

That's my offer.

Who's in?"

The President of Wilson shouted, 'I'm in' before anyone else could, Titleist came next then everyone followed.

"Thank you gentlemen. Please have your payments wire transferred to this account # at this bank in the Cayman Islands by tomorrow morning. He handed each man a piece of paper on which he had earlier scribbled the information they would need. We'll make the announcement following the championship ceremony tomorrow afternoon."

"The Cayman Islands?"

"That's right. Reba's Daddy is our banker. He does our day-to-day business in La Grange and the heavy lifting is in the Caymans. It works well for us."

"Goodnight partners. We'll see ya'll at the championship ceremony. Good luck to each of you and I sincerely mean it. I'd be disappointed if we won. It would ruin our everyman image."

In Santa Monica it was still early evening. Detective Garradelli and Detective Phillips had no problem rousting Eddie Ray out of his cell and summoning Larry Smyrle down to the jail.

"Good morning Mr. Smyrle we have a couple of questions for your client. The right answers could clear this whole thing up."

"Fire away.

Eddie Ray. They'll ask the question before you answer we'll talk. So do what your mama told you. Stop, look and listen before you cross the street. Got it?"

Eddie Ray nodded.

"How is it that Hudson James Camerman was in possession of your car last night?"

That question resulted in a long whisper fest between lawyer and client. Finally, Larry Smyrle spoke.

"We'll answer and you'll want to hear the answer but we want 'use' immunity for the answer."

"We figured you might. Here's a letter from the DA so stating. To be clear if you tell us something that we already know or could establish in some other way we'll come after your boy."

"Yeah, that's pretty much what 'use' immunity means. Let's go. Eddie Ray it's time to amuse the detectives with your tale."

"Leon and Candace had extorted a large sum of money from Mr. Camerman. They involved me to pick it up from him which I did for a 50% cut. There came a time when Mr. Camerman reconsidered his situation and decided to reverse the racket. He demanded twice what we had taken from him or he'd go to you guys. We believed him

He set up a meet for me and him in a secluded spot near Long Beach Harbor. I arrived in my triple black Lincoln, parked under a street light as I had been instructed and got out of the car with the duffle bag of cash in hand. There was no one and no other car around. Mr. Camerman stepped out of the shadows with a hand-howitzer sporting a silencer. It was the biggest gun I'd ever seen. Anyway, the guy told me to open the bag and dump out the money. Then he had me put it all back into the bag. Next, he had me completely and I mean completely disrobe and throw my pile of laundry to him. He threw me a set of gray sweats, a pair of jap-flaps and five bucks.

He had my wallet, my car keys, my cellphone and my gun. I had five bucks and some ill-fitting clothes.

Last time I saw Hudson James Camerman or my car was when he drove away with it was almost three years ago."

"Did you change your email address after that incident?"

"Not right away."

"You should have."

"Your story checks out with what we found in Mr. Cameron's car or your car as the case may be and what the widow Greenfeldt told us.

He had a gun similar to the one you described and a backup in the glove compartment which was registered to you. In the trunk we found, your wallet and your phone which was still getting copies of your texts and email.

That's how he learned about the casket full of cash plan.

We ran ballistics on his gun and it matches Mr. Greenfeldt's wound."

"Is my boy free to go?"

"He is, but we're gonna' come after him hard on any other extortion case we can make."

"Good luck with that. It's kinda' rare for a guy willing to pay hush money to suddenly get loud and talkative isn't it?"

"You never know. Hudson James Camerman did."

"Question detectives" Larry just couldn't resist.

"Shoot."

"How did Camerman do Greenfeldt?"

"We don't know for sure. Dead men tell no tales after all. What we can piece together is this. On the cash casket transfer day, he went to the Greenfeldt's house and convinced the maid to let him take one of the caskets. Mr. Greenfeldt was in the hospital and Mrs.

Greenfeldt was working another mark we think. Anyway, neither returned home until late and well after the maid had gone for the day.

Camerman tossed the empty casket into the back of his pickup truck and waited. You came and left with the cash casket. Greenfeldt followed you to make certain you made the drop. Camerman tailed him. Picture a parade. Greenfeldt parked in the alley near Milton's house. Camerman capped him, put him into the casket in the back of his pickup truck, pulled up behind your truck in Milton's driveway, took your casket and gave you his.

Two weeks or so after the La Grange burial you showed up in the dead of night discovered the switch which must have been a moment and reburied poor ole Leon.

That's what we think happened."

"How about my other client Mrs. Greenfeldt is she also free to go?"

"You can pick her up at the booking desk."

"Milton Muzny and Dave Holman are they off the hook as well?"

"Yeah, case closed. Hudson James Camerman gets full credit."

Larry called Guy.

Guy called Dave.

Dave called Milton.

Milton told Reba.

All was right in the world once again.

The next morning Milton woke up and paced. Reba was undisturbed as she was in another room. No ring, no proposal no fringe benefits.

He called the Cayman's spoke with his guy confirmed the transfers, all $500,000,000 million, half of which he transferred to the account of the Global Wildlife Foundation. Giving Herbert Anthony Franklin's authorization code he transferred half of that amount to Mr. Franklin's numbered account at the Rothschild Bank AG in Zürich, Switzerland.

"Milton, I heard you talking on the phone. Why are you up so early and what are you up too?"

"I was just checking on the status of our new best friends deposits. It's all there. Now we've got some real money to do some big things. Like **Chickenfried Café Frozen Food!**"

"That'd be interesting. First though you've gotta' expand our golf club production don't you?"

"I don't think so. Why compete with our friends? It might be best to let them take over the low end of the market and we'll go super high end.

We could always re-enter the market if the need arose by reducing prices."

"You're a real fart smeller Milton."

"I represent that!"

"The guys are ready to head out. That is everybody but Howard. He's as drunk as ten thousand Indians."

"Why?"

"Because he's a loser.

Some people are born that way and others sign-up for the role when they figure out that it's easier to be a martyr than a winner."

"No guts, no glory.

Are you going to pump him up and get him back into the game."

"No, I didn't take him to raise.

I'll probably leak the story about his condition to a reporter or two. That'll get us off the hook for his failure to appear and might even get us some good human interest press."

"Milton, you are hard as nails sometimes."

"Let's roll Baby Girl."

"They walked the course hand-in-hand from the 9AM tee time of their first player until the 6PM finish of their last, Chuck Bianchi."

"Well Reba we didn't win but we surely didn't lose. Now, let's do this press conference thing and head for the airport.

Is the plane there?"

"It is."

The Champions Cup and the big check went to one of Titleist's players. He spoke, they spoke and then Milton accepted the microphone.

"Ladies and gentlemen thank you very much for the enthusiastic support and the best wishes that you blew into the sails of the FiveOnFive Staff these past few days. I'll never forget it. We didn't take home the Championship and shouldn't have as it was never our goal. This tournament for us was always about you and the game of golf which has been dying for the last few years as interest swooned and should have. Our clubs have changed that. The game is now accessible to all. Grab a set and head for the golf course of your choice this weekend. Golf is your game and mine. Game meaning fun, not torture or embarrassment.

I'm not here to sell you a set of golf clubs. I'm here to sell you on the game of golf. Last night I entered into an agreement with all of golf's legacy manufactures. Each of them intends to bring our clubs to you with their secret sauce thrown in.

With our design and their manufacturing and distribution expertise I expect that golf will be the game of choice for all of America's families very soon.

I'll see you next year. Until then God's speed in whatever you do and where ever life takes you."

Milton and Reba waved goodbye to thunderous applause which was nothing even close to the welcome they received at the **Chickenfried Café's** home airport in La Grange, Texas. The ramp was filled with planes that had come from all over the state. The parking lot and even the sides of the highway were overflowing with parked cars and motorcycles that made the same trip. It was Milton's finest moment.

Reba was surprised when he whispered that he was going to have Arnold Bowles fly him over to the FiveOnFive Ranch so he could grab the *Texas Zephyr* and buzz the field at La Grange. She guessed that her man was intent on getting all of the publicity he could for everything that he was doing. It wasn't about golf clubs or chickenfried steak or airplanes. At the end of the day it was all about Milton.

Arnold landed and help Milton pull out the *Texas Zephyr*. Together they preflighted the electric beast. Milton said, "Arnold we gotta' hurry before the crowd thins out.

Tell you what; I'll give you a head start. When you get there put on a show but stay away from the strip. I'm gonna' come screaming down it going full tilt, then stand this bird on its tail and head straight up to fifteen thousand. Then I'll let the thing hammerhead and scream straight down to 500 feet before pulling up."

"Can the *Texas Zephyr* stand those loads?"

"Oh yeah! Not sure I can though."

Milton propped the Cub for Arnold and watched him crawl across the sky in the direction of La Grange.

As promised, the red dart that was Milton's *Texas Zephyr* came silently out of the sky, sailed past the crowd at five feet above the runway and stood on its tail just as he had told Arnold it would. Up, up and up it went until only those with the very best eyes could still strain enough to catch a glimpse of it.

Their reward was a bright flash followed by an orange ball of flame. Three seconds later they heard the sound of the explosion that would take Milton Muzny from them.

Where there had been a plane in flight heralding a new age of safe, fast electric air travel there was now only a shower of thousands of pieces of that promise tumbling slowly back to earth.

Guy Smyrle braced Reba as she tried to shield her eyes from what she was seeing and tried to force her mind to deny the reality she was now facing and would face for the rest of her days.

A piece of the machine met the earth just three hundred feet away and oddly and unbelievably began to roll and tumble towards Reba. It came to rest just ten from where she stood as frozen as a pillar. The brightly colored, shiny ring of titanium that just moments earlier had shielded the engine nacelle of the *Texas Zephyr* was now transformed into something much more important.

Soon it would be Monday. A new week would begin. Milton's Baby Girl finally had the ring he long ago promised.

Epilogue

St. Tropez is the best explanation life presents as to why it is better to be rich than poor. It is a magic place where the sun is forever warm and the people are always young. Beautiful shops, beautiful people, beautiful food, irresistible weather. St. Tropez is the cap on the bottle that holds the supreme wine we know simply as France.

It was a fitting place for Milton to be resurrected as Herbert Anthony Franklin.

"Should I call you Herb or Herbert or Anthony or.......
I have it, Tony."

"Bert, call me Bert."

"Bert how the heck did you get out of that exploding aircraft and why didn't anybody see your parachute?"

"Well, the fact is I was never in the airplane. The *Texas Zephyr* flew itself that day. It was among other things, a drone. It didn't need a pilot."

"How did you cause the explosion?"

"Pure science, Baby Girl, pure science, lithium-ion batteries have a tasty trait. When they are discharged too rapidly they overheat and explode."

"Is that what happened?'

"Patience Baby Girl. In this case, the batteries got really hot during the full power climb from sea level to fifteen thousand feet. The heat reached almost 900 degrees which was just enough to rupture the gas tank that sat on top of the battery module and ignite the fuel it housed.

That's what happened."

"Perfect!"

"By the way, Candace, if you're going to call me Bert, what shall I call you?"

ABOUT the AUTHOR

John Purner is an avid pilot, golfer, publisher, website developer and writer. For more than two decades, his **$100 Hamburger** *(www.100dollarhamburger.com)* website has been the world's most popular information source for recreational flying. John's first work of fiction, **02 Golf** has been an aviation category **Best Seller** since publication in 2011.

The following is a list of other John Purner books you may enjoy. They are available at Amazon.com and booksellers worldwide.

The $100 Hamburger - 2014/15

The $100 Hamburger Guide to Buying & Selling Aircraft

02 GOLF

6 Weeks to Winning Weekend Golf

BUYcycle: The Best Kept Secrets of Amazingly Successful Salespeople

15 BEST Airport Restaurants plus 2,347 Runner-Ups!

The $100 Hamburger – A Guide to Pilots' favorite FlyIn Restaurants 3rd Edition

101 Best Aviation Attractions

The $100 Hamburger – A Guide to Pilots' favorite FlyIn Restaurants 2nd Edition

The $500 Round of Golf: A Guide to Pilot-Friendly Golf Courses

The $100 Hamburger – A Guide to Pilots' favorite FlyIn Restaurants

www.ingramcontent.com/pod-product-compliance
Lightning Source LLC
Chambersburg PA
CBHW070954040426
42443CB00007B/497